# THIS BOOK BELONGS TO

Harry

*To the memory of my Grandmother, Margaret.*
*Without her, none of this would be possible.*
**E.J.**

*To Tom, who was born full of love and curiosity for nature.*
**A.W.**

First published 2018 by Nosy Crow Ltd.
The Crow's Nest, 14 Baden Place, Crosby Row
London SE1 1YW
www.nosycrow.com

ISBN 978 1 7880 0339 1

'The National Trust' and the oak leaf logo are registered trademarks of The National Trust
(Enterprises) Limited (a subsidiary of The National Trust for Places of
Historic Interest or Natural Beauty, Registered Charity Number 205846)

Nosy Crow and associated logos are trademarks and/or registered trademarks of Nosy Crow Ltd.

Text © Anna Wilson 2018
Illustrations © Elly Jahnz 2018

The right of Anna Wilson to be identified as the author and Elly Jahnz
to be identified as the illustrator of this work has been asserted.

A CIP catalogue record for this book is available from the British Library.

Printed in Italy

Papers used by Nosy Crow are made from wood grown in sustainable forests.

3 5 7 9 8 6 4 2

# 2019
# NATURE
# MONTH-BY-MONTH

 A Children's Almanac

Anna Wilson          Elly Jahnz

# WHAT IS AN ALMANAC?

The first almanacs were created about 3,000 years ago!
They were written by the ancient Egyptians who used
a kind of paper made from reeds known as papyrus.
The writers listed all the dates that were thought to
be lucky or unlucky, and made predictions about the
weather. Farmers used these almanacs to help them
know when to plant seeds and when to harvest crops.

Nowadays you can also find almanacs (like this one!)
which have fun facts about each month – things to
do indoors and outdoors, animals to spot, festivals to
celebrate and seasonal food to grow, cook and eat.
They also contain information about the weather,
the night sky and all sorts of other amazing facts.

## WARNING!

This book contains activities which involve
things like knives, saws, hammers and nails
and hot ovens. There are also a lot of fun
things to do outside which involve fire and
very cold water! All the activities are safe if
you are sensible, follow safety guidelines and
take a grown-up along to look out for you.

# CONTENTS

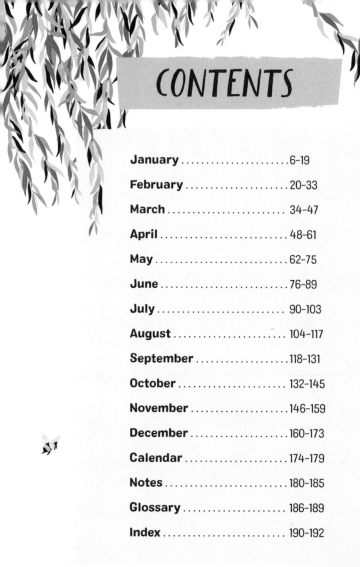

# January

## SPECIAL DAYS

**1st** New Year's Day/First Footing

**6th** Epiphany/Twelfth Night/
Wassailing

**13th** Lohri (Punjabi midwinter festival)

**21st** Tu B'Shevat (Jewish New Year)

**25th** Burns Night

# ANNIVERSARIES

**180 years ago ...**

On 9 January 1839 a French man called Louis Daguerre announced the invention of the *daguerreotype* – one of the first ever ways to create photographs.

**110 years ago ...**

On 9 January 1909 Sir Ernest Henry Shackleton led the famous Nimrod Expedition to plant the British flag 180 kilometres from the South Pole. This was the furthest south anyone had ever reached at this time.

> *"The blackest month of the year is the month of Janiveer."*

People often talk about January as though it is the worst of all the months.

"The sky is so grey!"

"It's so cold!"

"The days are so short!"

It's true that we don't see much daylight at this time of year. But wherever you live, you'll be able to find lots of things to get excited about in January. Yes, it's cold outside, but if you wrap up warm you can still enjoy walks and games and activities in the garden or park – or even by the sea. There are also some wonderful festivals in January which celebrate looking forward with hope to the year to come. So January's not that bad after all!

**Why is January Called January?**

The calendar we use today was invented by the Romans. January was named after the Roman god Janus who was the god of gates and doorways. He was always drawn with two faces looking in opposite directions – one face looked back at the year that had passed, and the other looked forward into the new year.

8

# DID YOU KNOW...

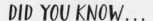

January used to have 29 days until the Roman Emperor Julius Caesar came along and named July after himself! Then the months had to be reorganised and January ended up with 31 days.

## New Year's Resolutions

On 31st December we often talk about 'making resolutions' for the new year. Why do we do this?

The tradition of making resolutions started with the Romans, too. Because the January god, Janus, was looking backwards and forwards at the same time, he became a symbol for the Romans of forgetting what had happened in the past and moving on into the future. January therefore became known as a month in which to forgive people and be kind.

Nowadays people seem to worry more about getting fit and not eating chocolate – maybe we should be more like the Romans and make resolutions to be kinder instead?

Here are some ideas for resolutions that you might manage to keep...

- Look out for someone at school who needs a friend.
- Have a cake sale or organise a sponsored silence or a sponsored walk for charity.
- Clear out your old toys and clothes and take them to a charity shop. (Check with an adult before you give these things away!)
- Help out around the house and/or garden, if you have one.

9

# FESTIVAL FUN

The colourful December festivals of light such as Christmas, Hanukkah and Diwali might be over, but January has its fair share of celebrations to look forward to.

### 6th January *Twelfth Night*

For Christians, Twelfth Night used to be the day when Christmas was celebrated. In some countries, 6th January is still the day on which children get their presents.

It is also known as Epiphany, St Nicholas's Day and the Feast of the Three Kings. For most people in Britain it's when the Christmas decorations come down, so it's not such a fun day.

### 6th January *Wassailing*

Wassailing is a pagan tradition. The word *wassail* comes from the Anglo-Saxon words *waes hael* which mean 'good health'. The festival is like many other winter celebrations in that it looks forward to what people hope for in the new year to come: good weather, good health and a good harvest.

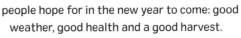

Wassailing involves going out into the countryside to bless the apple trees. The wassail king and queen lead everyone in a sing-song around the tree to encourage it to produce lots of apples.

The wassail queen sometimes climbs the tree and offers it some bread soaked in cider. You could make mulled apple juice to soak bread in instead.

## Recipe for *Mulled Apple Juice*

**You will need:**

Large saucepan
Wooden spoon
Ladle
Sieve
1 litre carton of apple juice
1 cinnamon stick

Zest of 1 large orange
Zest of 1 lemon
Small piece of root ginger,
peeled and grated
1 piece of star anise
2 teaspoons of runny honey

1. *Pour the apple juice into a large saucepan.*
2. *Put the cinnamon stick, orange and lemon zest and grated ginger into the juice.*
3. *Place the saucepan over a low heat and warm the juice, allowing it to simmer gently for about 10-15 minutes.*
4. *Stir in the honey.*
5. *Once the honey is melted, strain the liquid through a sieve while pouring it out into a heat-proof jug. The sieve will catch all the bits so you are left with only the yummy warm juice.*
6. *Serve in warmed mugs and drink it while it's still hot. Delicious!*

### 13th January *Lohri*

Hindus and Sikhs all over the world celebrate Lohri. During Lohri songs are sung to the sun god, Surya, thanking him for his warmth and praying for his return after the cold weather.

People drink *gurh* – a delicious sugary drink made from sugarcane. *Gajak* is also eaten – a thin, dry sweet made from roasted sesame seeds cooked in sugar syrup and spices. Children go from house to house singing folk songs and are given sweets. In the evening, a bonfire is lit and people gather together to dance.

11

# OUTDOOR ADVENTURES

It can be very hard to get up in the mornings in January. The sun doesn't seem to appear until school has begun – if it appears at all! But the dark mornings can be an exciting time for spotting wildlife. Even if you are not lucky enough to see an animal or bird, you might hear one instead if you listen hard.

Owls become very noisy at this time of year. You might catch sight of the large, silent shape of a tawny owl or a barn owl flying past you on your way to school.

Foxes and badgers are busy at this time of the year, too. They have to work hard to find food to keep them alive through the cold winter. Sometimes you can see them knocking over rubbish bins in their search for food!

If you go out into the garden, the park or the woods near where you live, you will see signs of new life even on the darkest day. In colder northern regions, plants take longer to appear, while down in the south you might see daffodils as early as 1st January.

Snowdrops are already in bloom in January. Their tiny white and green heads look so delicate, but they are strong enough to survive the coldest weather – even snow and ice!

Other plants are quietly peeping out of the damp, dark ground too. Hazel catkins can be seen hanging from the trees, even before the leaves start to show their shoots. Sometimes little yellow primroses start to appear now.

## How to Make a *Nature Notebook*

Take some sheets of scrap paper, fold them in half to make a booklet, then staple them together where you've made the fold.

Remember to make the notebook small enough to fit into a pocket so that you can take it with you wherever you go.

Tie a piece of string to a pencil and stick the loose end of the string into the notebook with sticky tape or make a hole in the pages and thread the string through. Use the pencil to note down where and when you see things while you are out and about.

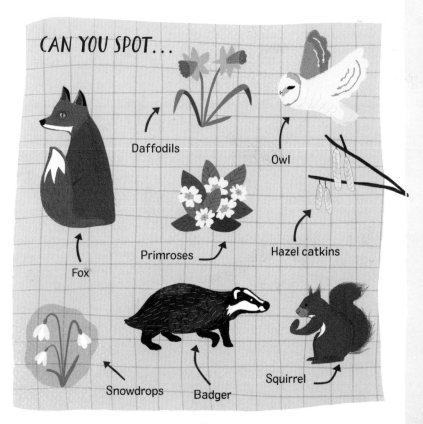

CAN YOU SPOT...

Daffodils

Owl

Primroses

Hazel catkins

Fox

Snowdrops

Badger

Squirrel

# BIRD SPOTTING

The RSPB holds a survey called The Big Garden Birdwatch at the end of January every year. This is to encourage people to record the different types of birds that regularly visit our gardens and streets so that we can keep an eye on their habits and see how the weather has affected them. More than half a million people get involved every year. Check the RSPB website to see how you can get involved. **www.rspb.org.uk**

## CAN YOU SPOT...

Blue tit

Coal tit

Long-tailed tit

Wren

Blackbird

Great tit

House sparrow

Robin

Starling

Magpie

Goldfinch

Wood pigeon

# GREEN FINGERS IN WINTER

The garden might seem empty and bleak in January, but there are still things you can do to get ready for spring. Maybe this will be the year that you have a go at growing your own vegetables? You don't need a garden to do this – you can grow things in pots or 'grow bags' which you can buy from garden centres or DIY shops.

Potatoes are a good vegetable to start with. In January you can buy potatoes to 'chit'. These are potatoes with shoots growing from them which will eventually grow into new potato plants. These small shoots need light and a cool temperature (about 4°C) to start them off.

Stand the potatoes in egg boxes on a windowsill in a cool room or garden shed, making sure that the ends with the most shoots are facing upwards. After about 4-6 weeks, the potatoes will have grown quite a bit. Wait until the shoots have grown to about 3 cm long and then you can plant them in the earth.

You can also plant a tree in January. How about asking your school if you could plant an apple tree? Or even start a small vegetable garden, beginning with those potatoes?

# GET COSY WITH AN INDOOR PICNIC

The long, dark evenings can be a time to get cosy and enjoy spending time with your family and friends playing games. Board games such as *Monopoly*, *Cluedo* or *Settlers of Catan* are perfect for January afternoons and evenings as they take a long time to play. A large jigsaw puzzle can be fun to do on a dreary afternoon, too. Make some mugs of hot chocolate, get into onesies or snuggle under blankets to make things extra cosy.

If you are feeling too sleepy to play games, you could just relax and have an indoor picnic instead. Get together some of your favourite snacks, lay out a rug and have your picnic straight away. Or you can spend the afternoon baking your favourite cakes, heating up sausage rolls and making sandwiches. You could put on a good film too, and turn your picnic into a 'movie night' with homemade popcorn.

## Make Your Own *Popcorn*

**You will need:**

**Large saucepan with lid
Large bowl for serving
3 tablespoons of sunflower
or groundnut oil**

**75 g popping corn
1 tablespoon of melted
butter
Salt and/or sugar to taste**

1 *Ask an adult to help you heat the oil in the saucepan on a high setting.*

2 *Once the oil is bubbling slightly, add two or three popcorn kernels to the pan.*

3 *When these kernels pop, add the rest of the corn to the oil in an even layer across the bottom of the pan.*

4 *Put the lid back on the pan and immediately remove the pan from the heat, but do not turn the stove off.*

5 *Count to thirty, nice and steadily. (Say, "One elephant, two elephants, three elephants," etc, so that you don't count too fast!)*

6 *Now put the pan back on the heat, keeping the lid on the pan.*

7 *The corn will start popping. Gently shake the pan by moving it back and forth on the heat to make sure all the corn pops.*

8 *Once the popping has slowed down to several seconds between pops, take the pan off the heat.*

9 *Carefully remove the lid and tip the popcorn into the bowl.*

10 *Pour the melted butter over the popcorn and add sugar or salt (or both!) to taste. Give the popcorn a light stir to make sure the butter and sugar or salt cover all the pieces.*

11 *Snuggle up, start the movie and enjoy!*

# THE NIGHT SKY

If there are no clouds, January is a great time for stargazing. As it gets dark so early, you can wrap up warm and go outside to look at the night sky.

Sometimes we see only part of the moon, depending on where the moon is in its journey across the sky. The different stages of this journey are called the 'phases of the moon'.

## *Phases of the Moon* in January 2019

**New Moon**
6th January

**First Quarter**
14th January

**Full Moon**
21st January

**Last Quarter**
27th January

The full moon in January is known as the Wolf Moon.

## The Seaside in Winter

The seaside is not an obvious place to go for a holiday or a day trip in the winter time. Just as the weather changes throughout the year, so does the temperature of the sea. In winter the sea temperature in Britain ranges from 6°C to 10°C. So it's a bit chilly for swimming and making sandcastles, and you can't exactly sunbathe! However, you can still hunt for shells and pebbles, seaweed and fossils, and you can look out for interesting seabirds and other creatures. A blustery coastal walk can be a lovely thing to do on a dull January day.

There are grey seals and common seals to be seen along the whole of the UK coast. In Cornwall and Wales you might also see porpoises. Along the seashore in Scotland, Northumberland, Yorkshire, Northern Ireland, and Wales you might also be able to see puffins.

## CAN YOU SPOT...

Sandpiper    Curlew    Gannet    Arctic tern

Black-headed gull    Common gull    Herring gull    Kittiwake

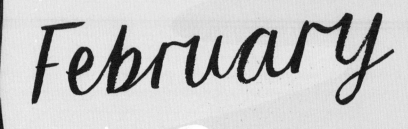

# February

## SPECIAL DAYS

**1st** Imbolc (pagan celebration)
**2nd** Candlemas (Christian festival)
**5th** Chinese New Year (Year of the Pig)
**14th** St Valentine's Day

# ANNIVERSARIES

**410 years ago ...**

In 1609, Galileo Galilei first looked at the sky through a telescope. His discoveries about space helped to explain to people that the Earth and planets in our solar system move around the sun. Before this, people believed that the sun and planets moved around the Earth instead!

> *"Surely as cometh the Winter, I know there are Spring violets under the snow."*

R. H. NEWELL (1836–1901)

February starts off cold and dark – at first it seems even more wintery than January! But by the end of the month we will have two hours more daylight and spring will be around the corner.

People often think of February as a time to be quiet and thoughtful before nature wakes up from its long winter's sleep. A few religions hold a 'fast' during this month, which means that people do not eat anything during daylight hours. Some Christians fast during Lent, which often occurs in February. Buddhists fast during a full moon. Some pagans fast in preparation for Ostara, the spring festival. The idea is that fasting helps you to clear your mind and focus on prayer.

By the middle of February, we can feel tired and in need of a break – so it's a good thing that the half-term holidays happen this month!

## DID YOU KNOW...

The month of Februarius had 28 days until around 450 BCE when it had 23 or 24 days every other year. Then Julius Caesar changed the calendar so that the month had 28 days and 29 every fourth year. This is how we got Leap Years. The next Leap Year is in 2020.

### Why is February Called February?

The Latin name for this month was *Februarius*. It came from the Latin word *februum* which means 'purification'. The Romans thought of the 5th day of this month as the first official day of spring. On the 15th they celebrated a festival called *Februa*.

This was a time to get rid of evil spirits and to cleanse the air so that people felt fit and healthy for spring. This is where we get our idea of spring cleaning from. Perhaps you could use the colder, darker days this month to tidy your bedroom or help clear out the shed or garage.

**Birth Flower and Birthstone**

Each month has a special flower and stone. February's flower is the violet. It is supposed to represent faithfulness, wisdom and hope, so anyone born in this month is said to be 'always true'. The stone is purple amethyst. The ancient Greeks believed that if you wore the stone, it would protect you from being poisoned! It is said to give you courage as well.

# FESTIVAL FUN

February is not all about fasting, cleaning and staying quiet. There are lots of celebrations happening all around the world, too. Some have serious meanings, but others are good fun!

### 1st February *Imbolc*

Imbolc (pronounced 'imulk') is a pagan festival. Its name comes from the Celtic word *imbolg* which means 'in the belly'. This is because nature seems to be expecting lots of babies at this time of year – baby animals, baby trees, baby flowers and fruit and vegetables. Everything is hidden away at the moment, but that doesn't mean nothing is happening deep in the cold dark ground – or inside pregnant animals! To celebrate, people sometimes make dolls made of corn called 'Bridey Dolls' which are said to bring good luck.

## 2nd February *Candlemas*

Candlemas is a Christian festival. It celebrates the day that the baby Jesus was taken to the temple for the first time. The festival always takes place on 2nd February and marks the end of the Christmas season. At Ripon Cathedral in Yorkshire, people celebrate by lighting 5,000 candles to symbolise Jesus bringing light into the darkness of the world.

## 5th February *Chinese New Year*

This year, Chinese people all over the world will be celebrating the Year of the Pig. There will be festivities in big cities throughout the UK. Chinese New Year is a noisy and colourful occasion. There are firecrackers, lion and dragon dances, music, parades, lanterns and special foods such as noodles. People wear red clothes for luck and to ward off evil spirits. People born in the Year of the Pig are believed to be patient and hard-working.

## DID YOU KNOW...

The noodles eaten at Chinese New Year symbolise a long life. Spring rolls represent wealth, and oranges and lettuce are for luck.

## 14th February *St Valentine's Day*

St Valentine's Day is an ancient tradition. Today, it's seen as a day to celebrate love. People send cards and flowers (particularly red roses), chocolates and other gifts. In some parts of Norfolk and Suffolk there is an old custom of leaving presents on people's doorsteps on St Valentine's Eve, the night before St Valentine's Day.

# THE SOLAR SYSTEM

The sun is in the middle of the solar system – the Earth and all the planets listed below move around the sun, and the moon moves around the Earth.

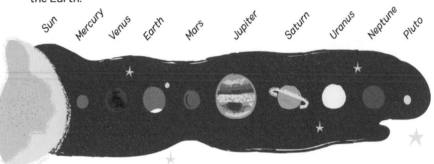

Sun    Mercury    Venus    Earth    Mars    Jupiter    Saturn    Uranus    Neptune    Pluto

## Constellation of the Month

Canis Major, or the 'Great Dog' can be seen this month. It chases Orion, the 'Hunter', across the sky. To find it, look for Sirius, the 'Dog Star'. In fact, this is two stars very close together which is why is it so bright. It is one of the closest stars to planet Earth.

## DID YOU KNOW...

You can actually see Mercury, Venus, Mars, Jupiter and Saturn with the naked eye, but they are so far away they look just like stars.

# WEATHER

## "When halo rings moon or sun Rain's approaching on the run."

This is an old country saying, and there is some truth in it. If you see a halo around the moon or sun at this time of year, it is because ice crystals can sometimes form in high clouds. These make a ring or 'halo' appear, and later these crystals may fall as rain. Rainy days can seem boring, but remember that the rain is doing a good job of watering all those tiny plants that are waiting for spring to arrive. Also, the rain comes from clouds which come in all shapes and sizes. Cloud spotting can be fun – what kind of pictures and shapes can you see in the clouds today?

## Cloud Spotting

Most of our names for clouds come from Latin. They are a combination of the following:

**Stratus/strato =**
flat/layered and smooth

**Cumulus/cumulo =**
heaped up/puffy, like cauliflower

**Cirrus/cirro =**
High up/wispy

**Alto =**
Medium level

**Nimbus/Nimbo =**
Rain-bearing cloud

Combining the names tells you a bit more about the clouds. For example: nimbus + stratus = 'nimbostratus'. This is a cloud which is flat and layered and will probably bring rain. 'Cumulonimbus' is a puffy cloud which will bring rain, too.

# GREEN FINGERS IN WINTER

There are lots of tidying-up jobs to do outside at this time of year to get the garden ready: so it's all about spring cleaning!

If you have a pond, you need to make sure it doesn't freeze over, as fish won't be able to breathe. You can stop the surface of the pond turning to ice by putting a tennis ball in the water – or even a rubber duck!

You can also get planting for next year. Why not put some snowdrop bulbs in the ground or in pots? Maybe ask your school if you can plant some. Mint grows well in pots too. It is delicious added to cooked peas or boiled new potatoes. Add it to a glass of iced sparkling water for a refreshing drink.

**Feed the Birds**

Small birds are hungry at this time of year. They need to eat all day to get enough food to keep them going through the winter. You can help by making your own treats for the birds using food scraps from home.

**Recipe for** *Fat Cakes*

**You will need:**

| | |
|---|---|
| Medium-sized saucepan | Washing-up gloves |
| Wooden spoon | Fat (lard or suet) |
| Large mixing bowl | Any of the following: |
| Garden string | Sultanas |
| Metal skewer | Porridge oats |
| Scissors | Bread or cake crumbs |
| Old yoghurt pots or large, dried, | Grated cheese |
| 'open' pine cones | Unsalted peanuts |
| | Wild birdseed |

*Mix one cup of melted fat with two cups of dry food.*
*If you want to make more, just double or triple the quantities.*

1. *Mix your dry ingredients together in a large bowl.*
2. *Melt the fat in the saucepan over a gentle heat.*
3. *Pour the melted fat over the dry ingredients.*
4. *Stir well until all the dry food is covered in the fat. The mixture should be nice and sticky. Let it cool slightly while you prepare the yoghurt pot or pine cone.*
5. *If you are using a yoghurt pot, make a hole in the bottom of the pot using a metal skewer. Thread a piece of string through the hole. The string should be long enough for you to tie it to a bird table or branch of a tree. Make a knot in the bottom of the string.*
6. *Fill the pot with the warm food mix, squashing it down with your fingers (wearing gloves) so that the pot is filled right up.*
7. *Place the filled pots in the fridge overnight to set.*
8. *Next day, cut through the pot and carefully peel it away from the hardened fat mixture.*
9. *You now have a fat cake ready to hang on a tree or bird table!*

## Pine cone variation:

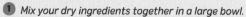

1. *Make the food mix in the same way.*
2. *Tie a length of string securely around the stalk end of the cone.*
3. *Scoop up chunks of the warm food mix with your fingers (wearing gloves) and squash the mix into the gaps in the pine cone, packing it in as tightly as you can.*
4. *Leave in the fridge overnight to set.*
5. *Next day, take it out and hang it up for the birds to enjoy!*

You will need help from an adult to melt the fat and to help you use the skewer and scissors.

# LET IT SNOW

Although we think of having a 'white Christmas', it's much more likely to snow in February in Britain. If it does this year, you won't have to think hard about the fun you can have outdoors. Everyone loves rushing out to make the first footprints in the snow, catching snowflakes on their tongue, having a snowball fight, sledging or building a snowman.

If you wrap up extra warm, you can make snow angels: lie down in a patch of freshly fallen snow and move your arms and legs up and down in the snow. Get up carefully and look at the pattern left behind – you've made a snow angel!

With a bit of help, you can also build a small igloo by packing the snow up into walls.

Or you can make snow bricks by using a spade to cut chunks of snow into cubes. Remember to leave a gap so that you can crawl inside.

You can also create wonderful snow lanterns by building a pyramid of snowballs and placing a tea light in the middle. Ask an adult to help you light the tea light and put it in the middle of your finished pile of snowballs.

# WILDLIFE ON THE MOVE

Toads, frogs and newts are often on the move in February. They walk and hop a long way to find others to breed with. The females then go on another long journey back to their ponds. They follow the same route, year after year. This sometimes gets them into trouble, as they cross roads, which were not there hundreds of years ago.

To help protect the amphibians from getting squashed, there are Toad Patrols up and down the country which go out in the evenings and pick the creatures up and carry them safely across the road. You can help amphibians to migrate safely by joining a patrol near you.

To find a Toad Crossing near you, go to **www.froglife.org** and follow the links. It's good fun and you can do some star-gazing and wildlife-watching too as foxes, badgers and owls are out in the evening as well.

## CAN YOU SPOT...

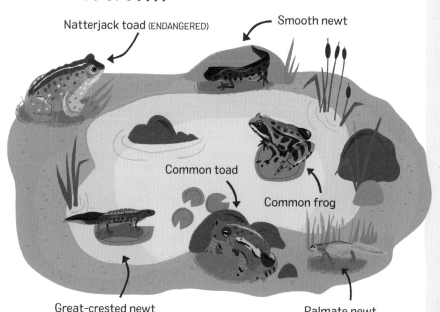

Natterjack toad (ENDANGERED)

Smooth newt

Common toad

Common frog

Great-crested newt

Palmate newt

# THE WEATHER OUTSIDE IS FRIGHTFUL

The half-term holiday can seem like a very long week if the weather is wet and windy, so it's a good idea to plan some indoor activities in case you can't get outside. Cooking is a great way to pass the time – and you can eat the results, so what's not to like?

## What's Growing Out There?

Many of the vegetables available in winter are not popular, I know. People often turn their noses up at turnips or beetroot or cabbage, for example. Maybe it's because they have only ever eaten them boiled. But there are so many other ways of cooking winter vegetables to make them tastier. You can even add some of them to cakes!

## Vegetables in Season

★ Parsnips, turnips, swede, celeriac, potatoes and beetroot – *can be roasted or made into vegetable crisps for a tasty snack.*

★ Kale, cabbage and spinach – *can be chopped and added to stir-fries and curries.*

★ Pears, apples and oranges – *are delicious raw, but can also be made into warming puddings such as cakes, crumbles and pies.*

★ Rhubarb – *is perfect for crumble, cakes and tarts.*

★ Leeks – *can be sliced or steamed or used to make a leek and potato soup.*

★ Cauliflower – *can be roasted in chunks (or as 'steaks') or in cauliflower cheese.*

### Recipe for *Chocolate Beetroot Cake*

It might sound weird, but this really is a yummy cake! The beetroot makes the cake squidgy like a chocolate brownie. Just make sure you buy the kind without vinegar as no one wants vinegar in a cake!

## You will need:

Sieve
20 cm x 30 cm baking tin
Food mixer or electric hand whisk
Wooden spoon
Spatula
Timer
Metal skewer
Kitchen paper

250 g pre-prepared, cooked beetroots, puréed
½ teaspoon of vanilla extract
300 g caster sugar
250 ml vegetable oil
3 eggs
225 g plain flour
1 ½ teaspoons of bicarbonate of soda
¼ teaspoon of salt
6 tablespoons of unsweetened cocoa powder

Ask an adult to help with anything hot or sharp!

1   *Put the beetroot purée in a sieve over the sink so that any extra liquid drains out.*

2   *Preheat the oven to 180°C/160°C fan/Gas Mark 4.*

3   *Grease the base of the baking tin using oiled kitchen paper and sprinkle some flour on top.*

4   *In a large bowl, mix the puréed beetroot, eggs, vanilla extract, oil and sugar. Use a food mixer or electric hand whisk on a low speed to mix everything well.*

5   *In a separate bowl, mix together the flour, bicarbonate of soda, salt and cocoa, using a wooden spoon.*

6   *Add the dry ingredients to the wet, beating everything together well.*

7   *Pour the batter into the prepared baking tin.*

8   *Set a timer for 50 minutes and put the tin in the oven.*

9   *Test to see if the cake is ready by poking a clean skewer gently into the cake – if it comes out clean, the cake is done.*

10  *Leave to cool on a rack, then turn out.*

You can ice the cake with chocolate icing or leave it plain. It makes a very good dessert with vanilla ice cream.

33

# March

## SPECIAL DAYS

**1st** St David's Day (Wales)

**5th** St Piran's Day (Cornwall)/Shrove Tuesday (Pancake Day)

**6th** Ash Wednesday (beginning of Lent)

**17th** St Patrick's Day (Northern Ireland)

**20th** Spring equinox (first day of spring)/ Ostara (pagan celebration)

**21st** Purim (Jewish festival)/Holi (Hindu 'festival of colours')

**31st** Mother's Day/Daylight saving (clocks go forward)

# ANNIVERSARIES

**130 years ago . . .**

On 31 March 1889, the Eiffel Tower opened in Paris. The tower was named after the engineer who designed and built it – Mr Gustave Eiffel. Many people didn't like the Eiffel Tower and said it was ugly! Today, more people pay to go up the Eiffel Tower than any other monument in the world.

# "March comes in like a lion, and goes out like a lamb."

This saying describes how March can be quite cold and blustery to start with, but by the end of the month it feels as though spring is in the air at last! After 20th March this year we will have one extra hour of daylight, when the clocks go forward. There will be many more flowers to see, the birds will be singing their hearts out and the baby lambs will be jumping about in the fields.

## DID YOU KNOW...

March is one of seven months of the year to have 31 days. Four months have 30 days and February only has 28 or 29 days.

## Why is March Called March?

The Romans called this month *Martius*. It was named after the god of war and farming. That might seem a strange combination, but both war and farming began again in March after the long winter months. Even soldiers didn't like getting cold and wet! The Saxons called March *Lentmonath*, which means 'lengthening month', because of the way that the daylight increases during this time. It is also where we get the word 'Lent' from.

## Spring Equinox

20th March is the spring equinox. This is one of the days in the year in which the number of hours of daylight is exactly equal to the number of hours of darkness. This happens because the rays of the sun are shining straight at the equator (the middle of the Earth).

*Phases of the Moon* **in March 2019**

| **New Moon** | **First Quarter** | **Full Moon** | **Last Quarter** |
| 6th March | 14th March | 21st March | 28th March |

37

# FESTIVAL FUN

Most festivals this month celebrate new life, hope and the arrival of spring.

**5th March** *Shrove Tuesday (Pancake Day)*

Shrove Tuesday gets its name from the ancient Christian practice of being *shriven*, which means being forgiven for things you've done wrong. It was traditional to tell a priest about anything bad you had done to get it out of the way before Lent, the season of fasting. Then, during the fast, you could concentrate on asking for forgiveness and promising to live a better life. On Shrove Tuesday, people used up eggs and fatty foods because during Lent they were not allowed to eat these things. One of the best ways of using up eggs and fat is to make pancakes, and a lot of people still do this today. That is why we also call this day Pancake Day.

## Recipe for *Mini Pancakes*

Why not do something different this Pancake Day and cook your pancakes outside? You can cook mini pancakes on an empty, clean tin can using a tea light for heat. Ask an adult to help. You'll need to make the pancake mix before you go outside. Take it with you in a sealed container.

### You will need:

Tin cans (washed, labels removed, and a few holes made with a skewer to allow air to flow)
Tea lights and a box of matches
Mixing bowl
Spoon
Wooden spatula
Kitchen paper
Paper plate

100 g plain flour
2 eggs
300 ml semi-skimmed milk
1 tablespoon of sunflower oil or vegetable oil (plus extra for frying)
Pinch of salt
Sugar, lemon juice – or whatever you like to have on your pancakes!

1  Put the flour and salt into the bowl. Make a dip in the centre with your fingers then crack the eggs into it.

2  Pour in 50 ml milk and 1 tablespoon of oil. Start whisking.

3  Beat until you have a smooth, thick batter. Add a little more milk if it is too stiff.

4  While whisking, ask someone to help pour in a steady stream of the rest of the milk until the batter looks as runny as single cream.

5  Once you are outside, lightly grease the base of the tin using oiled kitchen paper.

6  Light the tea light, put it on a flat, heatproof surface such as a paving stone, and place the tin over it. DO NOT TOUCH THE TIN – IT WILL BE HOT!

7  Spoon a thin layer of pancake mix on to the top of the tin and wait for bubbles to appear.

8  Carefully lift the pancake off with the spatula and turn it over.

9  When the pancake is cooked put it on a paper plate, add your favourite topping and eat!

Always blow the candle out when you're done!

# PANCAKE RACE

If you prefer to make your pancakes the 'old-fashioned' way in a frying pan, why not take things a step further and have a pancake race in your local park with your friends?

Dress up in silly costumes and see who can run the fastest while holding a pancake in a frying pan. Whoever drops their pan or pancake is out of the race. They are still allowed to eat their pancake – as long as it's clean!

### 20th March *Ostara*

Ostara is a pagan festival which is celebrated at the spring equinox. For pagans, it's a time of year when everything in the natural world is in perfect balance because the day and the night are the same length. The festival takes its name from Ostara or Ēostre, the goddess of renewal and rebirth. She has the head of a hare. Because hares are nocturnal (awake at night and asleep in the day) they are closely linked with the moon, as both come out at night. Hares also represent the rebirth of nature in spring.

## DID YOU KNOW...

Hot cross buns are thought of as an Easter treat because the cross on top looks like the Christian symbol. But long before Easter became a festival, pagans celebrated the spring equinox with Ostara buns that also have a cross on top. The round bun represents nature's 'Wheel of the Year', with the cross showing the four seasons.

## 21st March *Holi*

Holi is a Hindu festival also known as the 'festival of colours' or the 'festival of love', when Hindus celebrate the victory of good over evil and the arrival of spring. They meet to play and laugh, forget and forgive, and make up with people they have fallen out with! Holi lasts for a night and a day, starting on the evening of the *Purnima* (Full Moon day). People light bonfires and pray that evil will be destroyed. Then they smear each other with coloured paints and drench each other using water pistols and water-filled balloons! Imagine the world's biggest water-fight out in the streets, and that is Holi! Everyone joins in: friend or stranger, rich or poor, man or woman, children and older people.

## 21st March *Purim*

Purim begins on the evening of 20th and ends on the evening of 21st March. It is a Jewish holiday during which Jewish people remember that long ago their people were saved from Haman, a cruel man who worked for the King of Persia. At Purim, people have a big feast and send money and gifts of food to people in need. It is a time to think of others and be thankful for a good life.

# Recipe for *Ostara Buns*

## You will need:

Large mixing bowl
Small bowl
Baking tray
Silicone or greaseproof paper
Food mixer or wooden spoon
Piping bag and narrow nozzle
(and a very steady hand!)

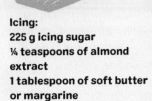

**Buns:**
900 g plain white flour
450 g caster sugar
110 g butter or margarine
200 g marzipan or almond paste
½ teaspoon of baking powder
1 teaspoon of cinnamon
5 medium eggs, beaten

**Icing:**
225 g icing sugar
¼ teaspoons of almond extract
1 tablespoon of soft butter or margarine
4 teaspoons of water

### Icing

1. Preheat the oven to 180°C/160°C fan/Gas Mark 4.
2. Mix the bun ingredients in a large bowl using your hands until a medium-soft dough forms.
3. Add a little flour if the dough is too sticky.
4. Break off small chunks of dough, about 3 cm across, and roll them into balls.
5. Place the balls on a baking tray lined with silicone or greaseproof paper, making sure they are not too close together.
6. Press each ball slightly to flatten the top.
7. Bake until golden brown (about 15-20 minutes) then set aside to cool while you make the icing.
8. Beat icing ingredients together in a food mixer or with a wooden spoon.
9. Put the nozzle in the narrow end of the piping bag and spoon the icing into the bag.
10. Hold the bag a few centimetres above each bun and squeeze out the icing to make a cross on top. If you don't have a piping bag you can drizzle the icing on top using a spoon.

# OUT AND ABOUT

There are more birds and animals to see in March. Some of them, such as chiffchaffs and wheatears, are visitors from other countries. It will depend where you live in the UK as to whether you are likely to see these birds. Some of them are found only in wetland areas or by the sea.

## CAN YOU SPOT...

| Chiffchaff | Sand martin | Sandwich tern | Blackcap |

| Chaffinch | Wheatear | Skylark | Lapwing |

## DID YOU KNOW...

Skylarks are tiny brown birds – not especially beautiful to look at. But their song is so gorgeous it inspired a famous piece of music called 'The Lark Ascending' by the English composer Ralph Vaughan Williams. You can easily find recordings of 'The Lark Ascending' online. Try listening to the music with your eyes closed: what do you imagine and how does it make you feel?

# HOW TO BUILD A NEST BOX

If you are going to make a nest box, you should complete it and hang it up early in March so that it is ready for the birds to start making their nest inside.

Nest boxes should always be made from wood. Metal and plastic are not good materials to use as they may mean that the nest will overheat or get wet and this will harm the eggs and the chicks. It is important that the inside of the box doesn't get too cold either.

### You will need:

★ **Short planks of strong wood, at least 15 mm thick (oak or beech is best as pine is rather soft and doesn't last as long)**
★ **Hammer**
★ **Stainless steel nails (not glue – nails allow water to drain out of the box)**
★ **Saw**
★ **Waterproof hinge for the lid (see page 45)**
★ **Helpful grown-up!**

### Follow the diagram below:

Make sure your grown-up drills a couple of holes in the base of your box so that any rain that does get in can drain out quickly.

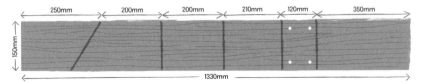

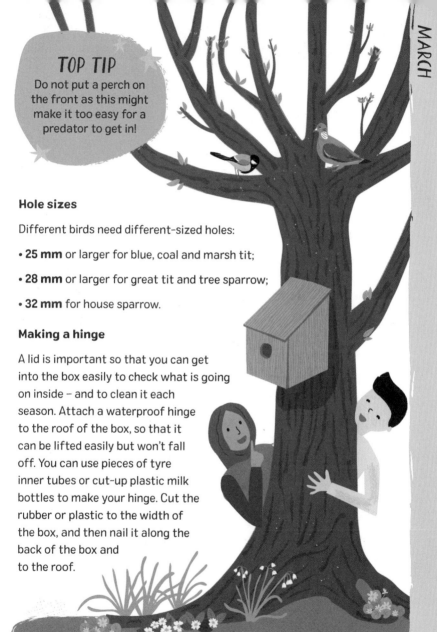

**TOP TIP**

Do not put a perch on the front as this might make it too easy for a predator to get in!

## Hole sizes

Different birds need different-sized holes:

• **25 mm** or larger for blue, coal and marsh tit;

• **28 mm** or larger for great tit and tree sparrow;

• **32 mm** for house sparrow.

## Making a hinge

A lid is important so that you can get into the box easily to check what is going on inside – and to clean it each season. Attach a waterproof hinge to the roof of the box, so that it can be lifted easily but won't fall off. You can use pieces of tyre inner tubes or cut-up plastic milk bottles to make your hinge. Cut the rubber or plastic to the width of the box, and then nail it along the back of the box and to the roof.

# DOWN BY THE RIVER

If you can get to a river, keep a sharp look-out for kingfishers. At this time of year the male bird is very busy, zipping along the surface of the water looking for fish – and a female to build a nest with!

You might also see a grey heron. They are large, serious-looking birds. Some people say they look like old professors! It is easy to walk right by one without seeing them, as they really do stand as still as stone statues.

**How to Skim a Stone**

'Skimming a stone' means throwing a stone across the surface of some water so that it bounces across the top without sinking straight away.

Once you have picked a stretch of calm water, you must find the perfect stone or pebble. The best 'skimmers' are flat and smooth.

Hold the stone loosely between your thumb and first finger. Tuck the other fingers underneath the stone to gently 'cup' it in your palm.

Hold your hand so that the front of the stone is pointing slightly upwards. Keep your elbow close to your body, then swing the stone from hip-height and whip your hand around.

## Skimming Scores

**Ratings Table:**

**0 bounces:** more practice needed!

**1-2 bounces:** good job

**3-4 bounces:** incredible

**5-6 bounces:** expert

**7+ bounces:** show-off!

The moment you let go, your first finger should be pointing in the direction you want your stone to go!

# WAKEY-WAKEY!

Creatures such as hedgehogs, dormice, bumblebees, butterflies and bats come out of hibernation at this time of year. They wake up from their long winter's sleep and immediately go searching for food to fill their empty bellies.

Maybe you have a tortoise as a pet? If so, you'll need to wake him or her up around this time. Wait until the outside temperature is at least 10°C before you move your tortoise outside, though. It will be a bit of a shock, moving from a cosy hibernation box to the chilly garden or patio!

# April

## SPECIAL DAYS

**1st**   April Fool's Day

**3rd**   Isra and Mi'raj (Muslim celebration)

**19th**   Passover begins (Jewish celebration)

**21st**   Easter Sunday (Christian celebration)

**23rd**   St George's Day (England)/
William Shakespeare's Birthday

# ANNIVERSARIES

**50 years ago . . .**

On 22 April 1969, the British yachtsman Sir Robin Knox-Johnston was the first person to go around the world by sea. He made the voyage on his own and didn't stop off in any countries on the way.

**55 years ago . . .**

On 21 April 1964, the TV channel BBC Two began showing programmes. Its first programme was a children's show called *Play School*.

# "Sweet April showers do spring May flowers."

THOMAS TUSSER (1524–1580)

People often moan about poor old April because it's a rainy month. One famous writer, T. S. Eliot, called it 'the cruellest month', but it actually has less rain in total than some other months. In any case, if we had no rain in April, those 'May flowers' would not 'spring' up!

It is true that April showers can be annoying. Those short, sharp bursts of rain seem to come from nowhere and disappear just as quickly. You have to remember to take an umbrella out with you in April even if the sun is shining when you leave the house! This is because the sky is full of cumulonimbus (those big puffy white clouds) which burst into rain and then clear away again to leave blue sky.

It can still be very cold in the mornings, too – you might see frost on the grass early in the day. There can also be heavy snow in the hills. So basically when you go out, be prepared for all weathers!

## Why is April Called April?

The Romans called this month *Aprilis* which came from the Latin word *aperire*, meaning 'to open'. Perhaps this is because flower and leaf buds start to open in April, as spring is finally here! The Anglo-Saxons called April *Ēosturmonath*, which means the month of the goddess Ēostre (or Ostara).

*Phases of the Moon* **in April 2019**

| **New Moon** | **First Quarter** | **Full Moon** | **Last Quarter** |
| --- | --- | --- | --- |
| 5th April | 12th April | 19th April | 26th April |

Do you know the difference between a new moon, a full moon and a blue moon?

A **new moon** is a moon we cannot see from Earth! This is because the moon is so close to the sun at this point, that the side facing us is in darkness. In other words, the moon is between the Earth and the sun and therefore is not lit up.

A **full moon** is when the complete circle of the moon can be seen in the sky. The full moon in April is called the Pink Moon.

A **blue moon** happens when there are two full moons in the same month. The last blue moon was on 31 March 2018, and the next one will be 2 October 2020. This is because the moon goes through all of its phases in 28 days, whereas our months can be 28, 29, 30 or 31 days long. So every two or three years, there will be a month or two in the year when there are two full moons.

### DID YOU KNOW...

The expression 'once in a blue moon' means 'very rarely' – this comes from the fact that it is a rare thing to see a blue moon.

# CONSTELLATION OF THE MONTH

Hydra, the water snake, can be seen from January through to May, but it is at its highest point in the sky in April. It seems to suit the rainy month of April rather well to have a water snake as the constellation of the month!

The story behind Hydra comes from Greek myths. One day the sun god, Apollo, sent a crow to fetch him a cup of water. When the mischievous crow came back, he gave Apollo a cup with a water snake in it instead! Apollo was so angry that he threw the snake and the crow into the sky and they became constellations of stars.

There is another Greek myth that has a monster in it called Hydra. This was a monster with many heads which the brave and strong hero, Hercules, had to kill.

# FESTIVAL FUN

### 1st April *April Fool's Day*

April Fool's Day is celebrated by people playing tricks on one another. Sometimes there are even April Fool's Day stories on the news. One of the most famous of these was in 1957 on the BBC television programme *Panorama*. The programme reported that in Italy there were spaghetti trees! Lots of people believed this because in 1957 not many people in Britain had eaten spaghetti, so they didn't know that it was made from flour and water and it definitely did not grow on trees . . .

> Can you think of any good April Fool's Day tricks?

## DID YOU KNOW...

There are a few unofficial rules about April Fool's Day tricks. The first is to do no harm – after all, the aim is to make someone look and feel silly. The second is that you can only play tricks before midday. If you try to trick someone in the afternoon, you become the fool!

# FESTIVAL FUN

**19th–27th April** *Passover*

Jewish people celebrate Passover to remember how the prophet Moses helped the Israelites escape from Egypt to a new life in the Promised Land. They left in such a hurry that the dough for their bread had not risen, so that is why Jewish people eat *matzo* at Passover today – a flat bread which is 'unleavened'. This means it has no yeast in it and so does not rise like a normal loaf of bread.

The Passover meal is called the *seder*. During the seder, Jewish families read and tell stories, eat special foods and sing songs, and children ask the adults questions about Passover.

**3rd April** *Isra and Mi'raj*

This festival is in two parts. The first part, the *Isra* or the 'Night Journey', starts on the evening before the day of celebrations. Muslims remember the prophet Muhammad's journey from Mecca to Jerusalem and then to heaven. Muslim people believe the Night Journey started when the Angel Gabriel took the Prophet Muhammad to Jerusalem on a winged horse, where he met and prayed with prophets including Moses and Jesus.

The second part is the *Mi'raj*, which means 'ladder' in Arabic. This was when the Prophet Muhammad was carried up to heaven by Gabriel where he spoke to Allah (God), who told the prophet that Muslims should say their prayers five times a day.

At Isra and Mi'raj, Muslim people say prayers during the night and Muslim cities keep their lights on all night.

### 21st April *Easter Sunday*

The Christian festival of Easter starts on the Thursday before Easter Sunday with a day called 'Maundy Thursday', when Christians believe that Jesus invited his followers to a meal called the 'Last Supper'. Easter ends on Easter Sunday when Christians believe that Jesus came back from the dead. It is a time for new life and rebirth. Easter eggs are also popular on this day.

## DID YOU KNOW...

The tradition for giving Easter eggs, which are a symbol of new life, comes from the pagan festival Ostara or Ēostre. The Easter Bunny, who is supposed to bring the eggs, also comes from the pagan religion, which has the hare as the symbol of new life.

# EGG–CELLENT ACTIVITIES

Today, a lot of people in Britain give and receive Easter eggs over Easter weekend, whether or not they celebrate any religious festivals.

**The Hunt is On!**

Easter egg hunts are always exciting. You could ask an adult to hide mini chocolate eggs outside in the garden or in an area of your local park or even while you are out on a walk. Then see how quickly you can find them – and don't eat too many on the way!

If the April showers are stopping you from going outside, why not have your Easter egg hunt in your home? There are plenty of places to hide eggs indoors. Make sure you find them all though – there's nothing worse than sitting on a forgotten Easter egg that someone has hidden under a cushion!

## Decorating *Eggs*

**You will need:**

**Hard-boiled eggs (cooled)**
**Wax crayons**
**Hot water**
**White vinegar**
**Food colouring**
**Different bowl for each colour**
**Tablespoon**
**Kitchen paper**

1. *Draw a simple design on the egg with a wax crayon.*
2. *Make dye by mixing 1 tablespoon of vinegar with 1 tablespoon of food colouring in a small bowl and add ¾ cup of hot water.*
3. *Place a hard-boiled egg on a spoon and lower it gently into the bowl.*
4. *Leave the egg in the dye for a few minutes.*
5. *Lift out the egg and place it carefully on a piece of kitchen paper.*
6. *As the egg dries, the pattern you drew will appear through the dye!*

**Make an *Easter Tree***

You can make a colourful Easter tree by hanging decorations on some twigs arranged in a vase. To make your tree extra special, you could paint your twigs gold or silver first. Or you could use sprigs of pussy willow, which are easily available at this time of year – and very pretty!

If you want to use your decorated eggs for this, you need to use uncooked eggs. Ask an adult to help you blow the yoke out first.

This is done by making a tiny hole in either end of the shell with a sharp pin, then the egg should be held over a bowl while the yolk and white is blown out of the egg into the bowl.

You now have an empty shell which you can decorate with dyes, paint or felt-tip pens.

# GREEN FINGERS IN SPRING

You don't need to have a vegetable patch to enjoy freshly picked food at this time of the year. The woods are full of wild garlic in April – the pretty white flowers look like little stars and the dark green leaves make yummy pesto sauce that you can eat

with pasta. The plant smells strongly of garlic, so it's easy to spot as you walk through the woods. You will probably smell it before you see it.

## TOP TIP
Never eat any plant unless an adult says it's safe!

**Recipe for** *Wild Garlic Pesto*

### You will need:

**100 g (a couple of handfuls) freshly picked wild garlic leaves**
**50 g pine nuts or hazelnuts**
**50 g parmesan cheese**
**1-2 tablespoons of olive oil**
**Juice of 1 lemon**
**Food mixer**
**Salt and pepper (if you like)**

1. *Pick the leaves from the wild garlic, making sure you don't pull up the little roots or bulbs of the plants.*
2. *Wash the leaves at home so that there is no grit or dirt on them.*
3. *Place the leaves, parmesan, olive oil and nuts into the food mixer and whizz them up until everything becomes a smooth green paste.*
4. *Add a bit more oil if you want the pesto to be runnier.*
5. *Add as much lemon juice, salt and pepper as you like. The lemon juice stops the pesto from going off too quickly.*

*Pop some on to your cooked pasta and mix it in. Yummy! Keep any leftover pesto in a jar and add a layer of oil on top to keep it fresh. You can keep it in the fridge for 3-4 days.*

# IF YOU GO DOWN TO THE WOODS TODAY

Woodland walks are wonderful in April. Not only can you go looking for wild garlic, you are very likely to see bluebells, too.

People used to believe that fairies used bluebells to trap humans who were out walking in the woods. You shouldn't go walking through the middle of a patch of bluebells anyway, as you may damage the bulbs and stop them flowering again.

A lot of butterflies come out at this time of year, too. They will be busy looking for flowers so that they can gather nectar to eat. See how many different kinds of butterfly you can find.

## TOP TIP
Bluebells are poisonous, so look, don't touch!

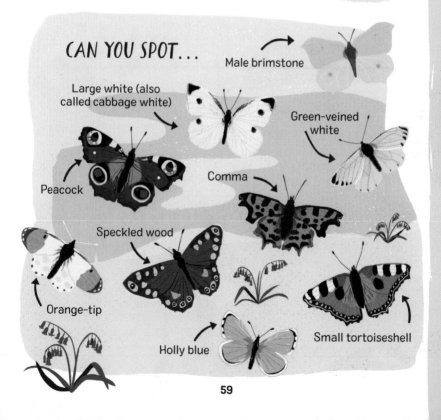

### CAN YOU SPOT...

Male brimstone

Large white (also called cabbage white)

Green-veined white

Peacock

Comma

Speckled wood

Orange-tip

Holly blue

Small tortoiseshell

# PARK LIFE

There's lots going on in local parks now that the days are longer and lighter. Why not join a park run? You don't have to be a fast runner, so you can chat as you run if you like! And there's often a park café nearby where you can go afterwards to have a well-earned snack and drink.

Look at the website **www.parkrun.org.uk** to find out where your nearest junior park run is. You will need to ask an adult to help you register online before you join a park run.

If running is not for you, take a scooter, skateboard or bike to the park. Or ask an adult if you can volunteer to walk a dog from your local dogs' home if there is one near you. (Or walk your own dog, of course!)

Whatever you choose to do, getting outside and breathing in the spring air will make you smile.

# BIRDS ON THE MOVE

The birds are getting noisier now! You might find that you are woken up earlier by the sound of a wood pigeon cooing loudly outside your window. Then other smaller birds join in with their different sounds. This is called the 'dawn chorus'. If you've got time in the morning, it's lovely to lie in bed and just listen to the music the birds make – it's like having a free concert right outside your window!

More and more birds are finding their way back to Britain after the winter. Look out for the first swallows, swifts and house martins later in the month.

Swallow

Swift

House martin

The bird that people think of most in April is the cuckoo. It spends the winter in Africa but comes back to Britain during this month.

Cuckoo

## DID YOU KNOW...

★ It is traditional for people to write to *The Times* newspaper when they hear the first cuckoo of spring!

★ Each spring a female will lay between 12 and 22 eggs, all in other birds' nests.

★ A female cuckoo will lay her eggs in a nest belonging to the same kind of bird that looked after her when she was a chick.

★ Adult cuckoos move back to Africa as soon as their chicks are hatched. This can be as early as the end of June.

★ Young cuckoos follow their parents back to Africa several weeks later.

# May

## SPECIAL DAYS

**1st** Beltane (pagan celebration)/ May Day

**5th** Ramadan begins (Muslim month of prayer and fasting)

**6th** Early May bank holiday

**27th** Spring bank holiday

**30th** Ascension Day (Christian celebration)

# ANNIVERSARIES

**500 years ago . . .**

On 2 May 1519, Leonardo da Vinci died. He is best known for his painting, the *Mona Lisa*, which hangs in the Louvre Museum in Paris. According to *The Guinness Book of Records*, the portrait is the most valuable painting in the world. Da Vinci didn't just paint – he was also a mathematician, a musician, an inventor, a sculptor, a writer, a map-maker and an architect!

# "We're cast a clout till May be out!"

This old country saying means that you should not rush to pack away your winter clothes until the month of May is over – or until the May flowers (also called 'hawthorn') are out in the hedgerows. This is because the weather can change quickly at this time of year. The air temperature is usually about 11°C–14°C, but in recent years it's become as hot as 25°C, as hot as a mid-summer's day!

It is tempting on days like this to run about in shorts and a T-shirt. But be careful – you might go out in the morning dressed for summer only to feel chilly by lunchtime when the clouds roll in. So if a grown-up tells you to take a jumper with you to the park on a boiling hot May morning, it might not be as silly as it sounds!

## Why is May Called May?

Nobody knows for sure, but it seems likely that this month was named after the Greek goddess Maia who was goddess of fertility. Her festival is still celebrated by some people on 15th May.

## DID YOU KNOW...

The Anglo-Saxons called this month *Thrimilci* (pronounced: 'Three Milky') because May was the month in which the cows were eating so much rich green grass that they could be milked three times a day.

## May Birth Signs

**Taurus** The sign of the bull. Some people believe that anyone with a birthday which falls between 20th April and 21st May is born under this sign. They are supposed to be sensible and good at making and fixing things.

**Gemini** The sign of the twins. Anyone born between 21st May and 21st June is a Gemini. They are supposed to be very chatty!

## The Sky at Night

This month there will be a full moon on 18th May. The full moon in May is known as the Flower Moon.

**DID YOU KNOW...**

The names for the full moons come from Native American culture.

## Meteor Shower *Eta Aquariids*

These meteors usually fall sometime between 19th April and 28th May. This year, you should be able to see the shower from the night of 6th May to the morning of 7th May. About 30 meteors will fall each hour. The shower is formed by particles of dust left behind by Halley's Comet. This comet has been known about since ancient times and is the only comet that can be seen from Earth without using a telescope.

If you want to see the meteor shower you will have to stay up late or get up very early! The best spot to see it from will be a very dark place from about midnight. The meteors can appear anywhere in the sky.

# FESTIVAL FUN

## 1st May *Beltane*

The old Gaelic word *Beltane* means 'bright fire'. This ancient pagan festival celebrates the return of summer and is also known as 'The Feast of the Good Fires'. It marks the time of year halfway between the spring equinox and the summer solstice.

Long ago, it was a time when farmers let their cows and sheep back out into the fields after the cold weather. To make sure that their animals would stay healthy, the farmers would light big bonfires and burn special herbs on them. They would then make their animals walk in between the fires so that they could breathe in the purifying smells. This was supposed to protect them from illness.

## 1st May *May Day*

May Day celebrations are often mixed in with Beltane bonfires. A May queen is chosen and either two people carry her, or she rides through the streets on a cart pulled by a horse. The cart is covered in flowers and the May queen wears flowers in her hair. She sometimes has a man or boy with her representing the Green Man, who is the pagan god of nature. People dance around a maypole which is a long stick with coloured ribbons coming from the top. Each person takes a ribbon and dances around the pole weaving in and out of each other until the pole is tightly wrapped in the ribbons. This is done to symbolise how the growing strength of the sun is finding its way into the land. Traditionally, May Day was a time for weddings and lots of parties.

### 5th May *Ramadan Begins*

The month of Ramadan traditionally begins
after the new moon, so the date for Ramadan
changes from year to year. During Ramadan,
Muslims hold a fast during the hours of daylight,
which means they are not allowed to eat or drink
from the moment the sun comes up until the
moment it sets. People must also try not to gossip
or fight during Ramadan. Muslims use the daylight
hours to focus on saying prayers and giving money
and possessions to charity. Some people try to learn the
whole holy book, the *Qur'an*, during this time!

## DID YOU KNOW...

'Hobby horses' are a May Day tradition. Originally a hobby horse
was not just a horse's head on a stick, like the toys you see
today. It was a costume for the May Day parade which made the
person wearing it look as though they were riding a real horse.

# MAKE A MINIATURE GARDEN

If you have one of those May days where one minute you are running around outside in the sun and the next you are running inside from the rain, you might like to try this.

You can wrap up warm to go and gather what you need, then come inside and stay cosy and dry while you bring a part of the outdoors indoors!

**TOP TIP**
Ask a grown-up before picking any flowers.

**You will need:**

**Old plastic tray, seed tray or biscuit tin lid**
**Small bowls to gather items for the garden**
**Soil or sand**
**Gravel or pebbles**
**Herbs and small flowers – rosemary, mint, daisies and buttercups are ideal**
**Tin foil (can be pre-used) or a small mirror**
**Moss or grass cuttings**

1. *Take your tray or tin lid and fill it with soil or sand.*
2. *Use the gravel or pebbles to make a path or to map out flowerbeds.*
3. *Take some moss or grass cuttings to make a mini lawn on some of the soil.*
4. *'Plant' the flowers and herbs in the rest of the soil as if you are making tiny flowerbeds.*
5. *Use the mirror or tin foil to make a pond or small stream.*
6. *If you wish, add plastic animals or other toy figures.*

Sit back and imagine whose garden it could be. Maybe you could write a story about your miniature garden?

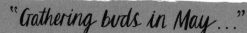

## "Gathering buds in May..."

May is the month for wild flowers. It seems as though nature finds any excuse to sprinkle the roadsides, paths, woodlands and parks with colour. Even the most boring motorway drive or train journey is made more enjoyable by looking out of the window at the burst of colour alongside the roads and railways.

Why not take your nature notebook with you and note down or draw what you see? You can also pick one of each flower that you find and then press it when you get home. Then you can stick the pressed flower into your nature notebook.

### How to *Press Flowers*

You don't need a special flower press. You can simply use paper and a very heavy book!

1. *Take some sheets of newspaper and the biggest, heaviest book that you can find.*
2. *Lay the flowers on the newspaper, opening them out as much as you can without breaking them.*
3. *Put another sheet of newspaper on top of the flowers.*
4. *Open the heavy book near the end.*
5. *Put the newspaper sheets into the book.*
6. *Close it and make sure the heaviest part of the book is on top of the flowers.*
7. *Leave for two or three weeks.*
8. *The flowers will have dried out and be pressed very flat. They will be very delicate so take extra care when lifting them off the newspaper.*

### TOP TIP

Use your dried flowers to make bookmarks or even add them to homemade paper.

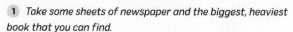

# WILD FLOWER SPOTTER'S GUIDE

See if you can spot any of these wildflowers in parks, on woodland walks or in the garden:

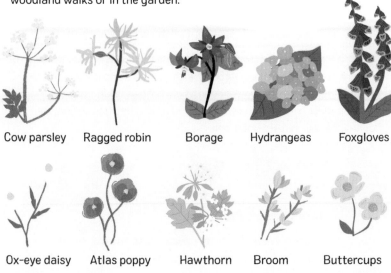

Cow parsley    Ragged robin    Borage    Hydrangeas    Foxgloves

Ox-eye daisy    Atlas poppy    Hawthorn    Broom    Buttercups

## Down by the River

If you can get to a river in May, you will see the water looking at its most beautiful. There is so much to see, so take your nature notebook with you! Water lilies start to bloom during this month and they attract pretty insects such as banded demoiselle damselflies.

Bullrushes grow tall along the riverbank, too, and you'll be able to see dragonflies hovering around them. There are lots of families of mallard ducks around at this time of year – see how many tiny ducklings you can spot. Some families have up to twelve ducklings and they can be seen swimming in a line behind their mothers.

# WILD SWIMMING

During the month of May the river loses its muddy brown look and becomes fresh and green. The sunlight pours into the water and you can see fish and water boatmen and frogs zipping about in the shallows. On a hot day, the river seems to call out to you: "The water's lovely – why don't you jump right in?"

'Wild swimming' – or swimming in natural water, such as rivers, lakes and waterfalls – has become more and more popular in recent years and people now realise that it is very good for your health. If you do feel like a dip, make sure you have an adult with you and always check that it is a safe area to swim in. It is not a good idea to swim where the water is flowing too fast, for example. And always check that you can get in and out easily.

Take a look at websites such as **www.wildswimming.co.uk** to get help and ideas on where to swim, or get hold of the excellent book *Wild Swimming* by Daniel Start, which has lots of information on where to swim safely in the UK.

# BABY WILD ANIMAL SPOTTING!

There are so many more animals around in May – many of them are babies. May is the perfect time for spotting young fox cubs or badgers. If you have ever watched *Springwatch* on the BBC you will have seen how active these animals are, particularly at night.

A simple way to try spotting wildlife at night is to dress in dark clothing and sit very quietly in the garden while the sun goes down. Foxes, badgers, hedgehogs and bats become more active in the early evening. They come out of their homes looking for slugs, worms and insects to eat. Now that the weather is warmer, there is a lot more food around!

## Hedgehogs

These lovely little animals are sadly becoming very rare. There are now less than half the number of hedgehogs in the wild since the year 2000. This is possibly because there are fewer hedges for them to live in as so many hedgerows have been replaced with fences. The other problem is traffic. Many hedgehogs are killed on the roads. Some towns have special 'Hedgehog Crossing' signs to warn drivers to go slowly and look out for the creatures.

If you would like to get a hedgehog sign to put up where you live, visit **www.britishhedgehogs.org.uk**

### TOP TIP
Tinned cat food is a favourite treat for badgers, foxes and hedgehogs.

## Bats

There are 18 different types of bat in the UK! They are all protected because, like the hedgehog, their numbers are falling. Bats are not dangerous – they are clean and sociable animals and they like to stay away from humans. If you find you have bats living in your house, do not worry. They will not chew wires or make nests and they do not spread disease, but you should ask an adult to contact the Bat Helpline to find out how to deal with the bats safely.

Visit **www.bats.org.uk** to find out more.

## CAN YOU SPOT...

Brown long-eared bat

Common pipistrelle bat

Brandt's bat

## DID YOU KNOW...

Although we say 'as blind as a bat', this is not true – bats can see well, just not far. Bats are also the only mammal that can fly. They have skin that stretches between their bodies and their arms, hands and finger bones to create their wings.

# EAT YOUR GREENS!

More and more fruit and vegetables are coming into season now. The vegetable of the month is asparagus. It is most delicious when simply boiled or steamed and then eaten with melted butter. The traditional way of eating it is with your fingers, so it can be quite messy! You can also wrap cooked spears of asparagus in Parma ham for a tasty treat, or dip them into boiled eggs instead of your usual toast soldiers. Yum!

## Recipe for *Asparagus Cream Pasta*

### You will need:

| | |
|---|---|
| 1 bunch of asparagus | 2 small saucepans |
| 142 ml double cream | Long-handled metal spoon |
| 2 garlic cloves, peeled but | Sieve |
| left whole | Blender |
| 50 g parmesan cheese, | Large saucepan |
| grated | Colander |
| 250 g tagliatelle pasta | Pasta bowls to serve |

1 Cut off the tough, 'woody' ends of the asparagus and put them in the food waste bin. Then cut the tips away from the stalks. You will use both.

2 Put the cream and the garlic in one of the small saucepans and heat it until it is boiling, then take it off the heat and use the spoon to remove the garlic from the cream. Keep the pan of cream to one side while you cook the asparagus stalks.

3 Bring some water to the boil in the other small saucepan. Put the asparagus stalks in the water and cook for 4–5 minutes. Then ask a grown-up to help you tip the stalks out into a sieve and pour the water away.

4 Put the stalks into the cream with the grated parmesan. Ask an adult to help you blend the stalks and cream using the blender until you have a smooth mixture.

5 Cook the pasta in a large saucepan, following the instructions on the packet. Throw in the asparagus tips 2 minutes before the end of the cooking time.

6 Gently reheat the blended creamy mixture.

7 Drain the pasta into the colander and tip it into the creamy mixture.

8 Mix gently, then serve in pasta bowls and top with more grated parmesan if you like.

## Birth Flower and Birthstone

Emeralds are the May birthstone. They are very rare gemstones and can be found in Colombia, Brazil, Afghanistan and Zambia. This rich green-coloured stone represents spring, rebirth and love.

Mayflowers, also called 'hawthorn', are the official flower of May. This white burst of blossom is seen up and down the country in the hedges and fields. It is a true sign that summer is on the way.

# June

## SPECIAL DAYS

**5th**    Eid al-Fitr (end of Ramadan)

**8th**    Queen's official birthday

**9th**    Shavuot (Jewish festival of weeks)/ Whitsun/Pentecost (Christian celebration)

**15th**    Trooping the Colour (the Queen's birthday parade)

**16th**    Father's Day

**21st**    Summer solstice

**24th**    Midsummer's Day

# ANNIVERSARIES

### 70 years ago . . .

On 8 June 1949, George Orwell's famous book *Nineteen Eighty-Four* was published. It predicted a world where we would all have TVs in our homes and and it would be possible to communicate via screens!

### 75 years ago . . .

On 6 June 1944, during the Second World War, 155,000 soldiers landed on the beaches of Normandy in France in the D-Day Landings.

# "June damp and warm does the farmer no harm."

Summertime is here at last! It's time for strawberries and cream and barbecues. The roses are out in the gardens and parks, and of course there are lots of long hot sunny days to look forward to – right? Well . . . there will be some sunshine, but often we get excited and plan summer outdoor activities in Britain, only to find that the rain means we have to change our plans.

Nevertheless, this is the month to enjoy long days outside. When you get home from school it feels as though you have so much extra time to have fun! You can meet your friends in the park for football or just laze around chatting in the shade eating ice cream. June has the longest day of the year, so by 21st June you won't see the sun go down until around 10pm. This will change depending on where you live in the UK.

## DID YOU KNOW...

On 28 June 1976, temperatures in Britain soared to 35.6°C! This was the hottest summer on record and there was a serious shortage of water that year.

**Average UK Day Length**

|  | SUNRISE | SUNSET |
| --- | --- | --- |
| **1st June** | 04:54 | 21:50 |
| **21st June** (Midsummer) | 04:45 | 22:06 |
| **30th June** | 04:49 | 22:06 |

## Why is June Called June?

The month of June was probably named after the Roman god Juno. She was the wife of Jupiter who was the king of the gods. Juno was the goddess of marriage. Some people think it is good luck to get married in June. The Anglo-Saxons called it *Sera Monath,* which means 'dry month'. (Maybe it didn't rain so much back then!)

## *Phases of the Moon* in June 2019

| **New Moon** | **First Quarter** | **Full Moon** | **Last Quarter** |
|---|---|---|---|
| 3rd June | 10th June | 17th June | 25th June |

## Constellation of the Month

Cassiopeia was a vain queen in Greek mythology. The legend tells us that she was thrown into the sky as a constellation after enraging Poseidon, the god of the sea. She boasted to him that her daughter, Andromeda, was more beautiful than his sea nymphs. She should have known that it is never a good idea to make an ancient god angry!

# FESTIVAL FUN

**5th June** *Eid al-Fitr*

Eid al-Fitr is an Islamic festival that is celebrated by Muslims all over the world. It is the day which ends Ramadan and it falls on or near the date of a new moon. During Eid, Muslim people celebrate with delicious food, by praying, and by giving money to charity.

**9th June** *Shavuot*

Shavout is a Jewish festival during which Jews remember the day that God gave the prophet Moses the holy scriptures, the *Torah*. All Jews go to the Synagogue on the first day of Shavuot to hear the reading of the Ten Commandments. This is a list of laws for living a good life. They can be found in the *Torah*, the *Qur'an* and in the *Bible* too.

### 9th June *Pentecost or Whitsun*

Pentecost or Whitsun is the eighth Sunday after Easter. On this day, Christians remember that God sent the Holy Spirit to be with the followers of Jesus. In Britain the festival borrowed some of the ideas from the May festival of Beltane, making it yet another celebration of summer arriving. In the north west of England some churches and chapels still hold 'Whit Walks' – parades that include brass bands, choirs and girls dressed in white.

**Birth Flower and Birthstone**

You have a choice this month between the pearl and the moonstone. Both are supposed to bring health and long life. The official flower of June is the honeysuckle. Bees, butterflies and birds love this sweet-smelling plant.

## DID YOU KNOW...

In Victorian times, people often grew honeysuckle flowers around the doors of their homes to ward off evil spirits.

# 21ˢᵀ JUNE SUMMER SOLSTICE

> *"In winter I get up at night*
> *and dress by yellow candle-light.*
> *In summer quite the other way*
> *I have to go to bed by day."*

ROBERT LOUIS STEVENSON (1850–1894)

It can be very annoying when you have to go to bed when the sun is still up! It is particularly hard to go to sleep on the longest day of the year. Pagans traditionally do not go to bed at all on this night! They stay up to welcome the sunrise and give thanks for its power and warmth.

One famous pagan summer solstice celebration happens at Stonehenge, a circle of standing stones in Salisbury in the west of England. People meet at the stones to watch the sunrise at about 4.45am. This is an act of worship and there is a lot of music and dancing.

The summer solstice is also known as *Litha*, which is an Anglo-Saxon word for 'midsummer'. Bonfires were lit on the tops of hills – some places in Britain still do this. The bonfire represents the strength, light and heat of the sun. Young men used to leap over them for luck!

# DID YOU KNOW...

In the North Pole, there is no night-time at all at midsummer. In fact, the sun remains in the sky for several days in a row! In the South Pole, the opposite happens – it stays dark for at least 24 hours.

### Morris Dancing

Morris dancing is a form of English folk dance with music. The dancers wear bell pads on their legs to add to the music and they use sticks and handkerchiefs. The sticks are clashed together in a pretend sword fight. The handkerchiefs are used to make the dance flow as the dancers wave them in the air. They wear white clothing with colourful ribbons and sometimes brightly coloured jackets as well. Music is played on accordions, concertinas, violins, flutes, tambourines and drums. Dances have names such as 'Cuckoo's Nest', 'Bean Setting', 'Bonny Green' and 'Hunt the Squirrel'!

### The Queen's Official Birthday

This is always celebrated on the second Saturday in June. The Queen appears on the balcony of Buckingham Palace in London to watch the Trooping of the Colour. The soldiers wear special uniforms to show which regiment they belong to. Music is played by the Foot Guards' Band and the Band of the Household Cavalry who are on horseback. There are 400 musicians in total!

The Queen gives awards called 'Birthday Honours' to people who have done something special in their lives, such as helping people in their community or charity work.

# STRAWBERRY FIELDS FOREVER

Who doesn't love fresh strawberries? They seem to burst on your tongue with the taste of summer sunshine. It is possible in some areas of the country to go to farms and 'pick your own', and that is the best way to get the freshest berries.

Strawberries grow very low to the ground in long rows. They are grown on straw to stop them rotting in the soil – which is, of course, how they got their name! To find your nearest 'pick your own' farm, go to **www.pickyourownfarms.org.uk**. You will be able to pick all kinds of fruit and vegetables yourself, not just strawberries.

## Recipe for *Strawberry and Shortbread Tart*

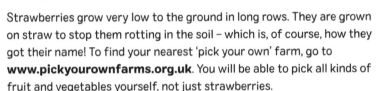

**You will need:**

**Food processor**
**Mixing bowl**
**Lemon-squeezer**
**20 cm loose-bottomed tart tin**
**(or a tartlet tin if you want to make small tarts)**
**Fork**
**Wire rack**

**Shortbread:**

175 g softened butter, cut into chunks
175 g plain flour
50 g cornflour or semolina
50 g caster sugar

**Topping:**

250 ml crème fraîche or whipped cream
1 tablespoon caster sugar
Juice of ½ lemon
1 kg strawberries (with leaves removed)
Icing sugar or caster sugar for sprinkling
Sprig of mint for decoration

1. Preheat the oven to 160°C/140°C fan/Gas Mark 3.
2. Grease the tart tin with a little butter.
3. Mix the shortbread ingredients using a food mixer.
4. When the mixture looks like fine breadcrumbs, tip it into the tin or tins.
5. Press it in firmly using your fingers.
6. Prick the shortbread mix a few times with a fork – this stops it rising up while cooking.
7. Cook for 40 minutes if you are doing a large tart or 15 if you are making smaller ones.
8. The shortbread is ready when it looks golden brown.
9. Take it out of the oven and let it cool on a wire rack.
10. Meanwhile mix 1 tablespoon of caster sugar into the crème fraîche or whipped cream and add as much of the lemon juice as you like – taste as you go!
11. Once the shortbread is cool, pile on the creamy mixture.
12. Finish by heaping on the strawberries and sprinkling with more sugar and a sprig of mint. YUM!

**WARNING!**
Ovens are hot!
Ask a grown-up
to help you and
wear oven gloves!

# LIKE A MOTH TO A FLAME

You will have seen how moths like to fly straight towards a light – they love it! It can be very annoying if you are trying to enjoy a meal outside with candles or if you have the window open on a summer's evening. However, if you are interested in observing moths close up, you can take advantage of their love of the light.

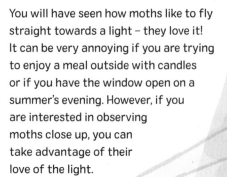

## How to Make a *Moth-Catcher*

1. *Hang a sheet up outdoors. If possible, make sure you hang it so that it is not near the light from your house. It is best to do this on a windless, dry evening. To make it easier to spot moths when they arrive, choose a light-coloured sheet.*

2. *Fetch a light which is bright enough to light up most of the sheet. A large torch set back from the sheet and shining up on to it will do the trick.*

3. *Turn on the light and wait for the moths to fly to your sheet! They will come almost immediately. Bring a camera and your nature notebook so that you can note down your findings and take some photos. Different moths will arrive at different times throughout the evening, so be patient!*

4. *Remember not to touch the moths and to leave them to fly off when they want to.*

### TOP TIP
To find out more about moths in the UK, visit
**www.ukmoths.org.uk**

# CAN YOU SPOT...

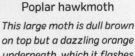

## Poplar hawkmoth

*This large moth is dull brown on top but a dazzling orange underneath, which it flashes when danger threatens.*

### Setaceous Hebrew character

*This is a very common moth. Look for the striking pale triangle which sits on either side of the wings.*

### Ruby tiger

*This moth is a beautiful bright red colour and has a cute furry head.*

### Elephant hawkmoth

*This moth is the most brightly coloured of all the moths found in the UK. They get their name from their large caterpillars which look like trunks!*

### Burnished brass

*This moth is a gorgeous mix of gold, bronze and brass colours with panels of greenish-yellow.*

### Garden tiger

*This moth has stunning spots and patterns on its wings. Its 'woolly bear' caterpillars are a favourite food of the cuckoo.*

### Green carpet

*This very small moth comes in many different colours and patterns. It rests with its wings laid flat to form a soft triangle shape.*

### Angle shades

*This moth is often mistaken for a dead leaf!*

### Antler moth

*This moth has a distinctive lightning-strike shape that branches off down either wing. You might even see this one during the day.*

87

# CARRY ON CAMPING

There is something very exciting about setting up camp in the summer, even if it's just in your own garden or in a park or field near your home. But it's not so exciting when the British summer lets us down by chucking rain on our tents!

If you are having a wet and miserable June this year, why not set up camp indoors? Ask an adult first, of course. In fact, you'll probably need an adult to help with this activity.

The best tent to use is a pop-up tent – the kind that you might take to the beach, for example – as these do not need tent pegs. If you don't have one of these, ask if you can use big cushions and blankets or a table and blankets to make your own 'tent' or den.

You can do this in any room where there is space. It's more fun if you don't do it in the room you normally sleep in, as that makes it feel more like camping!

## Making a *Table-Tent*

If you are using a table, cover it with a cloth or blanket that is large enough to fall to the floor. Then, when you crawl in, you shouldn't be able to see anything outside the table-tent.

Fill the table-tent with soft cushions and some of your favourite games or toys, then get duvets or sleeping bags to snuggle up in.

If you have some colourful lights, such as Christmas lights, string them up around the entrance to the tent – they can be your 'starry sky'! Then you can switch off all other lights in the room and use torches to see by when you are inside the tent.

**Campfire Food Indoors**

Ask if you can cook some sausages in the oven and make hotdogs to eat in your tent. For dessert you could try making 's'mores'. These are traditional American campfire treats made from marshmallows melted over the fire. The cooked marshmallow is then placed with a square of chocolate or a chocolate button between two crackers or biscuits. You can make them indoors by melting the marshmallows for a short time in the microwave in a bowl. Take them out carefully with a spoon and place them on a digestive biscuit with a piece of chocolate – they are just as yummy as the real thing!

## DID YOU KNOW...

S'mores get their name from the fact that they are so delicious they make you cry out, "I want s'more!"

# July

## SPECIAL DAYS

**12th**    Battle of the Boyne
(Northern Ireland holiday)

**14th**    Sea Sunday (Christian
celebration)

**15th**    St Swithun's Day

**25th**    St James's Day (Grotto Day)

# ANNIVERSARIES

**50 years ago...**

On 20 July 1969, humans first set foot on the moon! Neil Armstrong, Buzz Aldrin and Michael Collins were the crew members of the *Apollo 11* spacecraft.

## "Hot July brings cooling showers, apricots and gillyflowers."

SARA COLERIDGE (1802–1852)

The summer holidays start here, so you can start planning all the things you want to do now that you have no lessons or homework! The bright lime-coloured leaves become a deeper richer green and the wheat and barley fields turn golden. Lazy summer breezes ripple the long grasses, making the meadows look like green water. There are plenty of thunderstorms in July as well. But they usually don't last long.

When those fat raindrops fall on hot, dusty pavements they bring with them a gorgeous smell that you only get from summer rain. It's almost as though the Earth is sighing with relief at the chance for a long-awaited drink of water.

## Why is July Called July?

It was named to honour the Roman statesman Julius Caesar as it was the month in which he was born (12th July). Before that, it was known as *Quintilis* – Latin for fifth – as this was the fifth month in the Roman year before the calendar was changed. The Anglo-Saxons called it *Weodmonath,* which means 'the month of weeds' or *Heymonath* as this is haymaking time.

### Phases of the Moon in July 2019

| New Moon | First Quarter | Full Moon | Last Quarter |
|---|---|---|---|
| 2nd July | 9thJuly | 16th July | 25th July |

The full moon this month is known as the Buck Moon. Another name is the Thunder Moon because of the fact that there are often storms in the summer. Anglo Saxons called it the Hay Moon because of haymaking or Wort Moon as it's the time to gather herbs (or 'worts') for using as spices and medicine.

## DID YOU KNOW...

The Buck Moon gets its name from the new antlers that grow every summer from a buck (male) deer's forehead.

# THE MAN ON THE MOON

*"That's one small step for man,
one giant leap for mankind."*

NEIL ARMSTRONG (1930–2012)

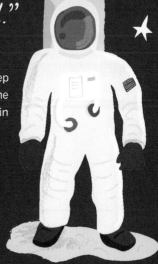

On 20 July 1969, the American astronaut Neil Armstrong was the first human being ever to step out on to the surface of the moon! He went to the moon on the spacecraft *Apollo 11* with Buzz Aldrin and Michael Collins. Neil Armstrong stepped out of *Apollo 11* at 10.56pm (EDT or 'Eastern Daylight Time') and Aldrin joined him about 20 minutes later. The men spent about two and a quarter hours together outside the spacecraft, and collected 21.5 kg of material to bring back to Earth so that the moon could be studied in more detail on their return.

## Top Five *Moon Facts*

1. The moon is the Earth's only natural satellite, which means that it travels around the Earth and it was not made by humans.

2. Scientists believe that the moon was made from bits of rock which were thrown into space when the Earth collided with Theia, an object which was about the size of the planet Mars.

3. As seen from the Earth, the moon is the second brightest regularly visible object in the sky after the sun.

4. The moon does not produce its own light. The reason it looks as though the moon is shining is because its surface reflects the light from the sun.

5. The moon also only ever shows us one side. The other side is known as the 'dark side of the moon'.

# DID YOU KNOW...

The moon affects the sea's tides. The tide changes every six hours, so if the tide is at its lowest (or the sea has 'gone out') at six in the morning, the tide will be at its highest again at midday. The tides change by about one hour every day. The reason the sea level changes throughout the day is because of the gravitational pull of the moon and the way the Earth turns. Tides change as the moon goes around the Earth and the Earth goes around the sun.

## Spring and Neap Tides

A 'spring tide' does not only occur in the spring time! It is the name for the highest tide of the month which in turn produces the lowest tide as its opposite. A 'neap tide' is the lowest high tide of the month and the highest low tide – this means that a neap tide shows the least difference between its high and low tides.

It is a good idea to check the tides before you go swimming or take a boat out on the sea. You can do this online or you can buy tide times booklets from your local seaside town.

# WHATEVER THE WEATHER

**15th July** *St Swithun's Day*

On St Swithun's Day there is a saying:

*"St Swithun's Day, if thou dost rain
for forty days it will remain
St Swithun's Day, if thou be fair,
for forty days 'twill rain nae mair."*

Thankfully, this is rarely true! St Swithun was
the Bishop of Winchester. When he died in 863 CE he
was buried in front of the west door of the old Saxon
cathedral building because he said he wanted to be
buried outdoors. He lay there for over 100 years. When
another bishop came along in 971 CE, he wanted to have
a new patron saint, so he dug up poor old St Swithun on his feast day,
15th July, and moved him to a tomb inside! That day there was a terrible
storm which lasted for 40 days and 40 nights. Many people believed
that this happened because the saint was not happy about being moved
indoors, so that is where the saying about the weather comes from.

**25th July** *St James's Day or Grotto Day*

There is an old tradition that on St James's Day, children would make
'grottoes' or little caves out of sea shells. This is because the scallop
shell is supposed to be the symbol for St James who was one of the
followers of Jesus.

Whitstable Oyster Festival begins on St James's Day. An old
Kentish tradition says that Julius Caesar went to Britain
because he loved the Whitstable oysters! The festival is a
celebration of thanksgiving that still survives today.

**Make a** *Seashell Grotto*

If you go to the seaside this month, you'll be sure to collect some shells from the beach. Why not make your own St James's grotto by the sea? Make a sandcastle and then decorate it with as many different kinds of shells and pebbles as you can find.

# SEA SHELL COLLECTOR'S GUIDE

Auger shell

Banded wedge shell

Cockle

Oyster

Crab shell

Common limpet

Common mussel

Dog whelk

Periwinkle

Razor shell

Shark's tooth

Slipper limpet

Sea potato

97

# OUT IN THE GARDEN

There are lots of jobs to do now that the weather is warmer. The most important job you can help with is watering the plants if there hasn't been enough rain. It is always best to do the watering in the evening because if the day gets hot, the water can evaporate too quickly and the poor plants can get burnt. Tomato plants and runner beans need a lot of water at this time of year. So do any flowers you have growing in pots.

Another fun job you can help with is picking fruit – just don't eat too much as you pick! Lots of berries and currants will ripen this month: gooseberries, redcurrants, blackcurrants and raspberries.

When you've finished all your gardening jobs, find a lovely cool spot in the shade to rest. If you have two trees which are close enough together, you could ask an adult to help you put up a hammock. If you don't have a hammock, you could make a canopy instead by tying some string between two trees and hanging a sheet over it. Put a rug or some cushions under the sheet and you have a beautiful, cool canopy where you can read a book or have an afternoon snooze – or relax with a glass of homemade lemonade!

# Recipe for *Homemade Lemonade*

There is nothing more thirst-quenching on a hot summer's day than a glass of homemade lemonade with lots of ice! Traditional lemonade is not fizzy like the kind you buy from the shops. It is made from a sugary lemon syrup topped up with tap water. You can of course use fizzy water if you prefer.

**You will need:**

Serrated knife
Food processor
Sieve
Wooden spoon
Large bowl

3 unwaxed lemons
140 g caster sugar
1 litre of cold tap water
(or fizzy water)
Ice or pre-frozen slices
of lemon or lime

**TOP TIP**
Make your lemonade look on trend by serving it in jam jars with paper straws!

1. Ask an adult to help you slice the lemons with the knife and throw the pips away.
2. Tip the sliced lemon and half the water into the food processor and blend until the lemon is finely chopped.
3. Hold a sieve over a large bowl and pour the mixture into the sieve.
4. Press the lemony mixture through the sieve with a wooden spoon to get as much juice as possible into the bowl.
5. Pour the rest of the water and the sugar into the bowl and give the mixture a stir.
6. Serve straight away in tall glasses with plenty of ice or add frozen slices of lemon or lime.

# RAINY DAY FUN

It is always a good idea to have some ideas ready for rainy days during the summer holidays. Perhaps while the weather is good you could use your time outside to collect flowers and herbs for making pot pourri. Put them in a vase or jug of water to keep them fresh, then on a rainy day you can spend the time indoors drying the petals and herbs. Pot pourri makes a great gift and lasts a long time, too.

## TOP TIP
Always check with a grown-up before you pick any plants or flowers.

## Make Your Own *Pot Pourri*

**You will need:**

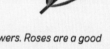

**Flowers**
**Herbs (rosemary, thyme or lavender)**
**Baking tray**
**Baking parchment**
**Scissors**
**One or two drops of an essential oil**
**such as rose or lavender**

1  Pick some of your favourite flowers. Roses are a good choice as they smell so good.

2  Preheat the oven to 100°C (or the lowest setting your gas oven has).

3  Cover the baking tray with baking parchment.

4  Cut the flowers from the stems right below the heads or place individual petals in a single layer on the sheet.

5  To add scent, cut and add herbs such as rosemary, thyme or lavender.

6  Add one or two drops of your essential oil to some water and sprinkle over the flowers and herbs.

7  Dry your flowers in the oven for at least 2 hours or until the flowers are dry but not burnt.

8  Remove from oven and give the petals a final brief sprinkle of essential oil.

9  Once cool, put the pot pourri in a bowl and leave in a room to make the room smell nice, or package it in a small cardboard box or paper bag to give as a gift.

## TOP TIP
If the scent fades, add another sprinkle of essential oil.

# CURIOUS CROP CIRCLES

July is the month when crop circles appear in some fields. They are best seen from high up. The circles are formed by the stems of crops being bent or trampled on. Sometimes the patterns made are incredibly detailed and complicated. They are often found near the ancient pagan standing stones at Stonehenge and Avebury.

Crop circles are formed overnight, and are usually spotted by farmers or passers-by the next morning. Some people believe that aliens come to Earth to make these patterns! However, they are actually made by human beings who go into the fields at night while no one is around. It is common to see crop circles appear after a night with a full moon.

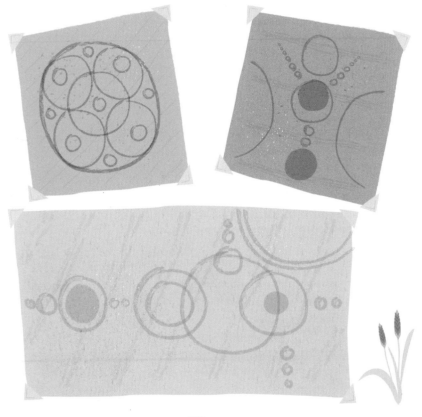

# DOWN ON THE RIVER

## Swan Upping

During the third week of July, the tradition of 'Swan Upping' takes place on the river Thames. This is a ceremony in which mute swans are caught by people in special boats called 'skiffs'. The swans are then 'ringed', which means they have numbered rings put on their legs so that we know how many swans there are. They are then released back to the river.

## River Clean-Up

There are 'clean-ups' in rivers all over the UK. These are organised events in which people come together to help clear away plastic and other rubbish which sadly finds its way into rivers and streams and causes all kinds of problems for the wildlife that lives there.

Getting involved in a clean-up is a lot of fun if you get together with your friends and make a day of it. The events often happen in secret natural spaces which you might not have been to before. It also gives you a chance to help save the environment and make life better for wild animals. You can take the plastic you find to recycling centres or supermarkets which will take plastic bags and film wrap as well as bottles and cans.

If you want to find a 'clean-up' near you, go to **www.ukrivers.net** and follow the links, or if you are near the Thames or any of the rivers and streams which flow into the Thames, look at **www.thames21.org.uk** for more information.

# August

## SPECIAL DAYS

**1st**    Lammas/Lughnasadh
(pagan celebration)

**5th**    Summer bank holiday (Scotland)

**12th**    Eid al-Adha (Muslim celebration)

**15th**    Raksha Bandhan (Hindu celebration)

**24th**    Notting Hill Carnival

**26th**    Summer bank holiday (England,
Northern Ireland and Wales)

# ANNIVERSARIES

### 80 years ago . . .

On 30 August 1939, an order was given that children from all the major cities in the UK must be sent to the countryside to be kept safe during the Second World War. The children were known as 'evacuees'.

### 200 years ago . . .

On 25 August 1819, the scientist, inventor and engineer James Watt died. He is famous for his work on developing the steam engine. He also created the world's first photocopying machine and he did a lot of work to help us understand energy, gases and electricity.

# "Dry August and warm Doth harvest no harm."

In August, it can feel as though the summer holidays will stretch on forever. You can enjoy the long, sunny days and spend as much time outside as possible. Perhaps you will be lucky enough to go to another country for your holiday, but if not there is more than enough to do closer to home. Days by the seaside or down by the river or playing in the parks or woods near your home offer lots of opportunity for activities and fun things to do with your friends and family.

Or perhaps you are the sort of person who likes to do nothing at all on a hot sunny day? Sometimes it's lovely just to find a spot of shade where you can read or snooze or sit and watch the world go by. Whatever you choose to do this August, make the most of all your free time and enjoy yourself!

## Why is August Called August?

The Roman Emperor Augustus Caesar thought that since there was a month named after his great-uncle Julius, there should be one named after him too! So *Sextilis* or 'the sixth month' was changed to August in the year 8 BC in his honour.

The Anglo-Saxons called it *Weodmonath*, which means 'weed month' as so many weeds grow at this time of year.

## Birth Flower and Birthstone

The flower for this month is the poppy which represents strength, love, marriage and family. The stone is called peridot. It is an unusual olive-green colour and contains a lot of iron. Peridot is formed in the magma of volcanoes and comes to the surface when volcanoes erupt.

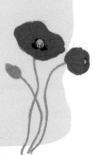

## Constellation of the Month

You can see the constellation of Pegasus in the east in the early evening. It is a square of four very bright stars with trailing 'legs' and a 'head' coming off it. The brightest of the four main stars is called *Epsilon Pegasi* and is an orange supergiant. The star's name in Arabic is *Enif* meaning 'nose' because it marks the place where Pegasus's nose is meant to be.

## DID YOU KNOW...

In Greek mythology Pegasus was a winged horse with magical powers. One myth says that he dug a spring of water out of the ground with his hooves. Anyone who drank the water was given the gift of writing beautiful poetry. Another myth tells of Pegasus going to the home of the gods on Mount Olympus, where he brought thunderbolts and lightning to Zeus, the king of the gods.

# CONSTELLATION VIEWER

If you can't get outside to look at the night sky, why not have a go at making your own constellation viewer? It is a good way of learning the different star patterns.

**You will need:**

**Constellation circles (see page 109)**
**Scissors**
**Plastic cup**
**Pencil**
**Glue**
**Drawing pin**
**Empty cardboard loo roll, kitchen paper or wrapping paper tube**
**Elastic bands**
**Sticky tape**
**Felt-tip pen**
**Chopping board (to lean on)**

1. Cut out each constellation circle using scissors.
2. Take a cup that is bigger than the constellation circle and draw around it to make a circle on a piece of paper. Cut out the circle.
3. Glue a constellation on each large paper circle.
4. Cut lines from the outside of the large circle to the edge of the constellation circle.
5. Use the drawing pin to make a hole where each of the stars is.
6. Put the paper disc on to one end of your tube, and hold in place with an elastic band.
7. Use sticky tape to stick the loose ends of the paper to the sides of the tube.
8. Write the constellation on the tube using a felt-tip pen.
9. Look through the empty end of the tube, pointing the constellation end towards the light – you'll be seeing stars!

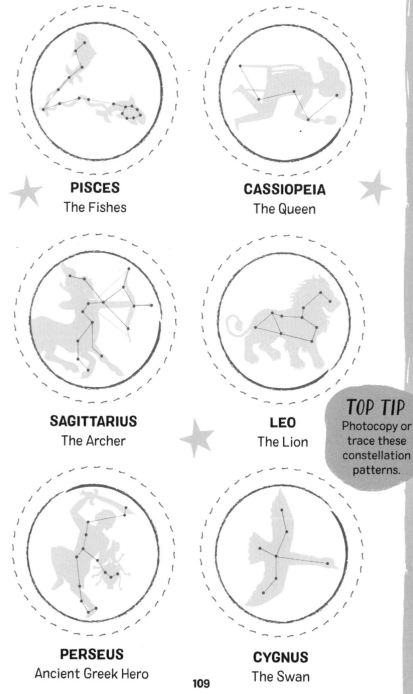

**PISCES**
The Fishes

**CASSIOPEIA**
The Queen

**SAGITTARIUS**
The Archer

**LEO**
The Lion

*TOP TIP*
Photocopy or trace these constellation patterns.

**PERSEUS**
Ancient Greek Hero

**CYGNUS**
The Swan

109

# FESTIVAL FUN

### 1st August *Lammas*

Lammas is a pagan celebration of the first harvest, and is a time for giving thanks. The word *lammas* comes from the phrase 'loaf mass' which is a special celebration of the first grain to be cut in the harvest, and the first loaf to be made from that grain.

Lammas is also the name of the grain goddess, harvest queen and Earth mother. The harvest god is called John Barleycorn.

### 1st August *Lughnasadh*

On this day there is also an old Celtic festival called *Lughnasadh* – the festival of *Lugh* or *Lug*, the Celtic sun king and god of light. The celebrations include feasting, market fairs, games, bonfire celebrations and circle dancing. This is a time to remember that the power and energy of Lugh (the sun) is now slowing down and the darker days of winter are just around the corner.

## DID YOU KNOW...

In the old days, once the last sheaf of grain of the harvest had been cut, the sheaf was made into a 'corn dolly' and carried through the village. If the harvest was good, the dolly was made into a pretty 'corn maiden' and if it was bad, it was made into an ugly 'corn hag'. How rude!

## 11th–15th August *Eid al-Adha*

This is an Islamic festival that marks the end of the *Hajj* pilgrimage to the holy city of Mecca. It commemorates how Ibrahim was willing to sacrifice his son Isma'il to God. Allah stopped the sacrifice and gave Ibrahim a lamb to kill instead. A version of this story is also found in the Jewish *Torah* and the Old Testament of the Christian *Bible*.

Many Muslims wear new clothes or their nicest outfits for this festival and attend a prayer service at a mosque. They also send Eid cards to family and friends, give money to charity, and give each other gifts.

## 15th August *Raksha Bandhan*

This is a Hindu festival celebrated at the full moon. The name *Raksha Bandhan* means 'the bond of protection'. The festival celebrates the relationship between brothers and sisters. During the festival, sisters tie a *rakhi* (a holy thread) around their brothers' wrists. The brothers in return vow to look after their sisters, and give them a present.

The best time to tie rakhi on Raksha Bandhan is during *Aparahna*, which is late afternoon.

## Recipe for *Buttermilk Bread for Lammas*

**You will need:**

Large mixing bowl
Wooden spoon
Measuring jug
Baking sheet
Greaseproof paper
Metal skewer
Knife
Coloured ribbon for
decoration – gold, orange
or yellow

550 g strong white flour
(plus extra for dusting)
1 teaspoon of
bicarbonate of soda
Pinch of salt
Handful of seeds
500 ml buttermilk (or
250 ml whole milk mixed
with 250 ml full fat Greek
yoghurt)

1. Heat the oven to 190°C/170°C fan/Gas Mark 5.
2. Place the flour, bicarbonate of soda, salt and seeds in a large bowl and mix well with your hands or a wooden spoon.
3. Make a dip in the centre with your fingers.
4. Pour in the buttermilk or yoghurt-and-milk mixture.
5. Mix well with a wooden spoon or your hands until the dough feels springy. If the dough is too sticky, just add a little more flour.
6. Turn the dough out on to a baking sheet lined with greaseproof paper and sprinkle with a fine dusting of flour. Then pat the dough with your hands until you have a round shape.
7. Take a knife and cut a cross into the top of your loaf so you have four sections, one for each season.
8. Place in the preheated oven for about 25-30 minutes. When the loaf is golden-brown, and a metal skewer stuck into the middle of the loaf comes out clean, the bread is ready.
9. Ask an adult to help you take the bread out and tap it on the underneath. If you hear a hollow sound this means that the loaf is done.
10. Now tie a bright ribbon around the loaf and share it with your family and friends. Eat it fresh, as soon as it is made if you can.

**WARNING!**
Ovens are hot,
so ask an adult
to help and wear
oven gloves!

# DID YOU KNOW...

Pagans give thanks before eating the Lammas loaf.
They turn it three times saying:

> "From the fields and through the stones,
> into fire, Lammas Bread.
> As the wheel turns may all be fed,
> Goddess Bless."

# GET WET!

**How to** *Build a Dam*

A hot summer's day is made much more relaxing if you can mess around in water. Building a dam is great fun and can be done by the river or even at the seaside – basically wherever a small stream of water is flowing gently. You'll need an adult to help you find the best place to build your dam.

Choose a narrow stream of clean, shallow water that you can paddle in safely. Once you have picked a good spot, start looking for driftwood, loose mud, rocks and pebbles. This will be your building material. You'll find the best bits and pieces at places where the stream bends, as rocks and things will tend to get stuck there.

See if you can stop the stream from flowing or change its direction by building up your dam. Where does the water go?

## DID YOU KNOW...

Humans build dams to control water so that it can be used for farming and to supply homes, schools and businesses. This is how reservoirs are made.

Beavers also build dams! They do this to make a pond of deep, quiet water where they like to build their homes or 'lodges'. The dams slow the flow of the water so that the beavers' homes do not get washed away.

# ROCK POOLING

If you can't find a stream, head to the seaside and splash around in rock pools to cool down. The best time to do this is at low tide on a calm day when the sea has gone out and left water behind in the dips and hollows between the rocks. There's a lot to see in these miniature underwater worlds, so make sure you take your nature notebook with you – and try not to drop it in the water! Take a net and a bucket too – that way you can take a closer look at some of the sea's minibeasts.

Remember to always be kind to the creatures you find and return them to their rock-pool homes after you have looked at them.

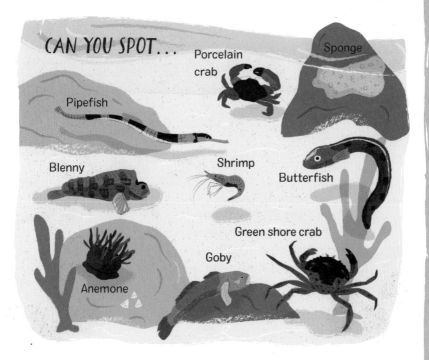

CAN YOU SPOT...

Porcelain crab

Sponge

Pipefish

Blenny

Shrimp

Butterfish

Green shore crab

Goby

Anemone

# FLYING-ANT DAYS

Flying-ant days usually happen around this time of year. They are not something that most people enjoy as it seems as though suddenly the sky is full of flying ants and they get everywhere! However, this is a very important time in the life cycle of the ant. It is the time when ants mate and fly away to start new colonies. Once the ants have mated, the females lay their eggs and create a new ant colony which they look after for the next year.

It is amazing how all the ants in one area seem to know when to take to the skies – as if they're reading the weather. If there has been some rain followed by a hot, dry period with light winds, the ants decide this is the day to take flight.

## DID YOU KNOW...

Although there is not one single day when the ants take to the skies, the numbers of ants flying seem to grow and grow to the point where it feels as though all the ants in the country have decided to fly off on the same day.

### Get Picking!

By the end of August there is often a chill in the early mornings which tells us that autumn is around the corner. Some of the autumn fruits are already starting to ripen. Look out for blackberries, bilberries and elderberries. You will be competing with the birds and field mice if you want to pick them, as these berries are a favourite food for wildlife too!

Bilberries

Blackberries

Elderberries

# Recycle for *Blackberry and Apple Crumble*

**You will need:**

Large mixing bowl
Medium saucepan
Wooden spoon
Medium ovenproof pie
or flan dish

**Topping:**

120 g plain flour
60 g caster sugar
60 g unsalted butter,
cut into small chunks
25 g of demerara sugar
for sprinkling

**Filling:**

300 g Bramley apples,
peeled, cored and chopped
30 g caster sugar
115 g blackberries, washed
¼ teaspoon of ground
cinnamon

1 Heat the oven to 180°C/160°C fan/Gas Mark 4.

2 Tip the flour and butter into the mixing bowl.

3 Lightly rub the butter into the flour using your fingertips until the mixture looks like breadcrumbs.

4 Stir in the sugar and put the topping in the fridge while you make the filling.

5 Put the peeled and chopped apple in a saucepan with the blackberries and cinnamon and sugar.

6 Heat through on a medium heat on the stove for about 5 minutes until the blackberry juices have started to run.

7 Tip the fruit mixture into the pie or flan dish.

8 Add the cold topping and finish with a sprinkle of demerara sugar.

9 Cook in the preheated oven for 30–40 minutes.

10 Serve with vanilla ice cream, crème fraîche or natural yoghurt.

## WARNING!

Ovens are hot, so ask an adult to help and wear oven gloves!

# September

## SPECIAL DAYS

**1st** Start of autumn/Muharram (Islamic New Year)

**2nd** Ganesh Chaturthi (Hindu festival)

**23rd** Autumn equinox

**23rd** Mabon/Harvest festival

**29th** Michaelmas Day (Christian celebration)

**30th** Rosh Hashanah (Jewish New Year)

# ANNIVERSARIES

**Over 350 years ago . . .**

On 2 September 1666, a fire broke out at a bakery on Pudding Lane in London. The fire quickly spread and destroyed much of the city. Remarkably, only a few people died in the Great Fire of London, and the city was rebuilt very quickly.

> *"September days are here,*
> *With summer's best of weather*
> *and autumn's best of cheer."*

HELEN HUNT JACKSON (1830–1885)

September can be a golden month. Summer is fading, yes, but there is still warmth in the air, and the leaves on the trees are slowly turning from their different shades of green to the fiery colours of autumn. And, of course, the end of summer means the beginning of school again, which not everyone is happy about! But the days are still long enough to allow some time for fun in the park after school, so make the most of it before the clocks change and the countdown to winter begins.

## Why is September Called September?

This month kept its original name from the Roman calendar. September comes from the Latin word *septem,* which means 'seven'. September was the seventh month in the year when the calendar began with March instead of January.

## Constellation of the Month

*Cygnus* means 'swan' in Latin. The Romans took the word from the Greek *kyknos*. The ancient Greeks had many stories about swans. One of them was about the tragic hero Orpheus. He was killed and then transformed into a swan, after which he was placed in the sky. The constellation of Cygnus is quite easy to spot as it is shaped like a cross. It is in fact sometimes known as the Northern Cross.

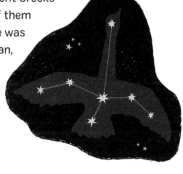

## September Birth Signs

People born from 23rd August to 22nd September are said to be born under the sign of Virgo. They are supposed to be loyal, kind, hard-working and practical. They can also be worriers, are often shy and can end up working too hard if they don't make time to relax. They like animals, reading and nature and they don't like rude people! (Who does?)

People with birthdays on or between 23rd September to 22nd October are born under the sign of Libra. The sign is depicted by a set of weighing scales which represent a balanced personality. Librans are lovers of peace and harmony. Unfortunately, this means that they sometimes can't make up their minds as they can usually see both sides to every argument!

121

# FESTIVAL FUN

If you found it hard to stick to your New Year's Resolutions, you could try starting again in September! This month is a time for new beginnings for some religions. It is also time to give thanks for nature's gift to us of the harvest.

### 1st September *Muharram*

Muharram is the Islamic New Year. The Islamic calendar is based on phases of the moon, and is 354 days long. This means that the date of the start of Muharram changes every year. During the month of Muharram, many Muslims fast and pray.

### 2nd September

## *Ganesh Chaturthi*

Today is the day that Hindus start celebrating the birthday of Lord Ganesha, the god with the head of an elephant. Communities get together to worship, have parties and decorate their houses with models and pictures of Lord Ganesha. He is known as the god of new beginnings and is supposed to bring prosperity, good fortune and success.

### 23rd September *Mabon or Harvest Festival*

The harvest festival is the closest thing we have to a day of thanksgiving in Britain. The word 'harvest' comes from the Old English word *hærfest* meaning 'autumn'. This was a very important time of year, as the success of the harvest could mean the difference between life or death for a whole community. In the past, even children had to help bring in the harvest. Then, as soon as it was over, everyone would return from the fields for the Harvest Supper. This was a huge feast with much singing and laughter.

## DID YOU KNOW...

The 'gleaning' was the act of collecting any crops leftover in the field. This was done by the women.

## 29th September *Michaelmas Day*

The Christian celebration of Michaelmas, or the 'Feast of St Michael and the angels' falls near the equinox. Traditionally Michaelmas Day was the time when new servants were hired or land was bought or sold, and money was paid back to people who had lent it. This is why most schools and universities start their new year around September, some of them even call the autumn term 'Michaelmas Term'.

## 30th September *Rosh Hashanah*

This is a very important Jewish festival as it celebrates the start of the New Year in the Hebrew calendar. It is also a time for giving thanks for the birth of the universe and the day on which God created Adam and Eve. People light candles, enjoy special meals and come together to pray.

# BONKERS FOR CONKERS

'Conkers' is the name of a traditional game that is played using the seeds from the horse chestnut tree.

## Prepare Your Conkers

1. *Choose two of the biggest, smoothest, roundest conkers you can find.*
2. *Ask an adult to make a hole through the centre of each one, either with a nail or a screwdriver, or even a drill.*
3. *Take two long pieces of string or garden twine – about 20 cm long – and thread a piece through the hole in each conker. Make sure you tie a knot in the bottom so that the conkers don't just slide off!*
4. *Find a friend and challenge them to a game . . .*

## How to Play

★ Stand opposite each other, holding the end of the string so that the conkers are hanging down.

★ Take it in turns to hit your conker against your opponent's.

★ The conker that breaks the other one gains a point.

## Scoring

★ If you have a conker that has never been used in the game before, it is called a 'none-er' because it has not got any points yet.

★ If a 'none-er' breaks another new 'none-er' conker, it becomes a 'one-er'.

★ If it was a 'one-er' and it breaks another conker, it becomes a 'two-er', and so on.

★ If the strings get tangled up during play, the first player to shout "Stringsies!" has an extra turn.

**TOP TIP**
When playing, hold the conker low, away from your face, and never flick or throw a conker near someone else's face.

# WILD SEA, WILD ME

Believe it or not, September is the best month to go for a swim in the sea. This is because the water has been warming up over the summer and it is now as warm as it will be all year round. If you do fancy a dip, take a grown-up with you and be careful to check the tides beforehand. Make sure you are swimming in a safe area where you can get in and out easily. Also take a good look at the waves first, as the sea can begin to get quite stormy and rough in September.

# FOOLISH FOR FRUIT FOOL!

This month is a wonderful time to gather in your own mini-harvest. You can either go foraging in the wild for blackberries, or you could find out where to pick your own raspberries or damsons (a type of small plum). Why not try making a 'fruit fool'? Fools are easy to make and somehow bring the last taste of summer along with them.

## DID YOU KNOW...

The dessert used to be called a 'foole'. No one really knows where the name comes from. Some people think it is from the French word *fouler*, which means to crush or press, as the fruit is mashed up when it is stewed.

**Recipe for** *Fruit Fool*

## You will need:

Medium saucepan
Wooden spoon
Metal spoon (if using
damsons)
Hand whisk or electric
whisk
Spatula
Glass bowl or individual
glasses

500 g soft fruit or berries
100 g caster sugar
200 g double cream
100 ml thick Greek-style
yoghurt or crème fraîche

① Wash the fruit carefully, then put it with the sugar in the saucepan over a low heat, stirring occasionally.

② Cook until the sugar has dissolved and the fruit has softened.

③ Remove from the heat and allow to cool.

④ If using damsons, take the metal spoon and pick out the stones. It is easier to do this once the fruit is cooked!

⑤ Whisk the double cream until it has formed soft peaks.

⑥ Gently stir the yoghurt or crème fraîche into the whipped cream using the spatula.

⑦ Add the fruit to the creamy mixture and stir.

⑧ Put the finished fool into a glass bowl or individual glasses or dishes.

⑨ Place the bowl or glasses in the fridge and leave for at least 2 hours so that the fool will set.

⑩ Serve with shortbread for a delicious end-of-summer dessert!

# CASTING ANIMAL PRINTS

September is a lovely time of year to go for a walk in the woods. It's also a perfect time to look out for animal and bird tracks as the ground is becoming softer after the drier summer months. Creatures leave traces of where they have been in the mud and leaf mould. If you go prepared, you can take a cast of any tracks you find and take it home as a souvenir. You have to be very patient if you want to find the prints that animals and birds leave behind. Ask a grown-up to help you with this activity. You'll need to carry your equipment in a small bag or rucksack.

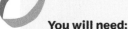

**You will need:**

**Small bowl**
**Circle made from cardboard or bottom of an old plastic bottle**
**Plaster of Paris (be sure to read the instructions!)**
**Spoon (old one!)**
**Small bottle of water**

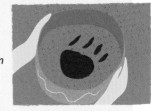

1 Put the circle of card or plastic around the animal print. Make sure there are no gaps between the bottom of the circle and the ground or the plaster of Paris will leak outside the circle.

2 Ask an adult to help you mix up a small amount of plaster of Paris with some water using the spoon and the bowl.

3 Pour the plaster into the circle above your print. Leave for 10-15 minutes or according to plaster of Paris instructions – perhaps go and find another animal print while you wait for it to dry!

4 When the plaster is dry, remove the circle and you should have the shape of your animal or bird track sticking out of the plaster.

128

**5** *Take it home and paint the paw print or bird print. Use the tracker guide below to identify the print.*

**Animal Print Guide**

Badger

Deer

Squirrel

Duck

Fox

Otter

Hedgehog

Rabbit

Dog

*Phases of the Moon* **in September 2019**

| First Quarter | Full Moon | Last Quarter | New Moon |
|---|---|---|---|
| 6th September | 14th September | 22nd September | 28th September |

**Harvest Moon**

The full moon in September is known as the Corn Moon or Harvest Moon, depending on when it appears in the month. It is called the Harvest Moon before the 23rd September, or the Corn Moon after.

# CREEPY CRAWLIES

Poor old spiders have got quite a bad name for themselves – so many people are scared of them! We shouldn't be frightened of them in Britain, though, as they are not dangerous and in fact they are very useful and do a lot of good.

## Six Spidery Facts

★ People think there are more spiders around in the autumn, but actually it's just that we're more likely to see them at this time of year. This is because some choose to come indoors as it gets cooler outside, and also because it's the mating season, so the males can be seen hurrying around trying to find a female.

★ Spiders don't particularly like baths – and they definitely don't like getting wet. It's just that they sometimes fall in and then can't climb out! This is especially true of large spiders which, unlike some smaller ones, can't walk up smooth surfaces.

**TOP TIP**
Try leaving strips of loo paper hanging into the bath to help trapped spiders climb out!

★ All British spiders use poison to digest their prey. However, they are not harmful to humans – and they couldn't bite you, even if they tried because their fangs are too small or weak to puncture our skin.

★ We live alongside so many spiders that we are never more than a metre away from one! Most are very small, so you probably won't even see them.

★ Very few spiders enjoy living in modern centrally-heated homes. Most of them would prefer us to take them back outside as they really like living in garages or sheds where they can hide in peace and quiet.

★ You might not like having spiders around, but they are useful because they eat other bugs that we also dislike. They are particularly keen on midges and mosquitoes. So remember – it would be a lot worse if there weren't any spiders around.

## DID YOU KNOW...

*Arachnophobia* means 'a fear of spiders' – it comes from the Greek words *arakhnē* (spider) and *phóbos* (fear).

## CAN YOU SPOT...

False widow

Cave spider

Money spider

Black lace weaver

Lace webbed spider

Garden spider

House spider

# October

## SPECIAL DAYS

**9th**    Yom Kippur (Jewish holiday)

**21st**   Apple Day

**27th**   October Daylight Saving/Diwali
(Hindu New Year)

**31st**   Samhain Eve (pagan festival)/
All Saints' Eve (Christian festival)/
Halloween

# ANNIVERSARIES

### 40 years ago . . .

On 12 October 1979, the famous comedy science fiction book by Douglas Adams called *The Hitchhiker's Guide to the Galaxy* was published.

### 50 years ago . . .

On 14 October 1969, the British fifty-pence coin came into use. It replaced the ten-shilling note.

# "Corn and grain, corn and grain. All that falls shall rise again."

WICCAN HARVEST CHANT

October leads us gently into autumn. The days are still mild and the light is golden as it reflects off the turning leaves. The colours are glorious! This is the perfect time of year to go out walking in the countryside and parks. Run through the fallen leaves and look out for especially beautiful colours and shapes. Maybe you could collect your favourite leaves and press them? Pressed autumn leaves make brilliant decorations on cards or bookmarks.

## DID YOU KNOW...

The American word for autumn is *fall*, from the expression the 'fall of the leaf' or the 'fall of the year'. The word 'fall' was actually used in Britain instead of 'autumn' for a long time. It wasn't until people began to use the French word *l'automne* in the 18th century that we let go of the word 'fall'.

## Why is October Called October?

October gets its name from the Latin word *octo* which means 'eight', and was named by the Romans during a time when the calendar year began with March instead of with January as it does now.

The Anglo-Saxon name for this month was *Winterfylleth* which comes from the words for winter and the full moon.

*Phases of the Moon* **in October 2019**

| **First Quarter** | **Full Moon** | **Last Quarter** | **New Moon** |
|---|---|---|---|
| 5th October | 13th October | 21st October | 28th October |

## The Moon's a Balloon!

The October full moon this year is called the Hunter's Moon. It is also known as the Blood Moon because it can often be a striking red or orange colour. Of course, the colour of the actual moon hasn't changed! The moon hangs lower in the sky at this time of year, closer to the horizon, and so we are seeing it through more of the Earth's atmosphere. The gases around the Earth and the tiny particles in the air affect the way in which we see light. Orange and red light has longer wavelengths and so these are the colours we see reflected off the moon when it is closer to us.

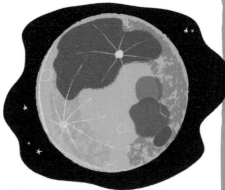

You can see the moon's craters much more clearly at this time of year. These have been caused by objects crashing into the moon from space.

# FESTIVAL FUN

### 9th October *Yom Kippur*

This is the holiest day of the year for Jewish people. It is a day for saying sorry for things you have done wrong and asking for forgiveness. Jews traditionally wear white and they fast and pray for up to 25 hours. They often spend most of the day in the synagogue.

### 27th October *Diwali*

Diwali marks the start of the Hindu New Year. Sikhs and Jains also celebrate at this time. Diwali is five days long, and on the third day, many Hindus light special oil lamps called *diyas*. The lamps symbolise the triumph of light over darkness, good over evil and knowledge over ignorance. Many gods, including Rama and his wife, Sita, and Lakshmi, the goddess of wealth and prosperity, are celebrated with music, *puja* (prayers), firework displays and by sharing traditional sweets.

### 31st October *Samhain Eve*

The festival of Samhain (pronounced "Saah-win" or "saah-ween") comes from ancient pagan Celtic and Gaelic harvest traditions. Its name means 'summer's end'. It is a time for giving thanks for the end of the harvest and it marks the beginning of the coldest half of the year.

Pagans celebrate by holding a feast and by remembering those loved ones who have died and are no longer with us. Sometimes people set a place at the table for these loved ones and put food in front of it as an offering to those who have passed on.

### 31st October *All Saints' Eve*

This is a Christian festival also known as All Hallows' Eve, Hallowed Evening or Holy Evening, which is how we get the name Halloween! On the evening of 31st October, some Christians begin three days of ceremonies and services to remember loved ones who have died and the saints ('hallowed' or holy people). It is traditional to light candles for those who have died and to spend time praying and remembering those people who have passed away.

### 31st October *Halloween*

Nowadays we associate Halloween with fun and games and dressing-up. But in fact, as far back as the 16th century, people had parties on 31st October, playing games and practising rituals to try and tell the future, especially about deaths or marriages in the family. This is where the game of apple-bobbing comes from, it used to be that the first person to bite into an apple was the first person to get married!

Before pumpkins were brought over from America, people would use turnips or other root vegetables to make lanterns. These were carved with ugly faces in the hope that they would scare away evil spirits.

# TRICK OR TREAT

It can be fun to get dressed up and go trick-or-treating around your neighbourhood. People usually let you know if they are happy for you to knock on the door by leaving a pumpkin lantern outside their homes. Or why not have a Halloween party instead? You can have a prize for the best Halloween costume and there are lots of great games you can play.

## I Want My Mummy!

This is a simple game that doesn't require any preparation. You will need one loo roll per team, and if possible you'll need a minimum of three people in each team – one to be the mummy and two to wrap him or her up!

Ask an adult to be your time-keeper. When the adult says "GO!" the other two team-mates have five minutes to wrap the mummy in the loo roll. The winning team is the one to do the neatest wrapping!

## Apple Bobbing

**You will need:**

**Large plastic washing-up bowl**
**As many apples as guests (stalks cut off so no one can cheat!)**
**Towel for people to dry their faces afterwards**

To play the game, take it in turns to put your face in the water and try to bite into an apple. The first person to bite an apple and pull it out of the water using only their mouth, or the person to get the most apples out of the water, is the winner.

## Yucky Dip

This needs preparation before the party.

**You will need:**

**3 packets of jelly in spooky orange, purple and green colours**
**Sweets such as Dolly Mixtures or Fruit Pastilles**
**Large see-through Pyrex or plastic bowl**

★ *Make the first jelly according to the instructions on the packet and mix in some sweets. Let this first layer set.*
★ *Make the next layer and add sweets in the same way.*
★ *Once this second layer has set, make the third layer and add the remaining sweets.*

To play the game, take it in turns to put your face in the jelly and pull out sweets. No hands allowed!

## Chocolate in Flour

**You will need:**

**Large plates**
**Packet of flour**
**Large bar of chocolate, broken into squares**

To play the game, take it in turns to put your face in the flour and pull out a square of chocolate. If you've played the Yucky Dip first, you might need to wash your face after this game. No hands allowed!

# Recipe for *Spooky Pumpkin Muffins*

## You will need:

12-hole muffin tray
12 paper muffin cases
Large mixing bowl
Wooden spoon
Dessert spoon
Spatula
Metal skewer

### TOP TIP
It can be a tough job, scraping out a pumpkin! If you use a spoon instead of a knife, it is easier and safer. You can also buy puréed pumpkin in tins instead.

## Muffins:

425 g puréed pumpkin
3 large eggs, beaten
350 g plain flour
120 ml vegetable oil
270 g caster sugar
2 teaspoons of baking powder
1 teaspoon of baking soda
pinch of salt
1 teaspoon of mixed spice

## Icing (optional):

60 g unsalted butter, softened
150 g cream cheese
350 g icing sugar
1 teaspoon of vanilla extract

1 Preheat your oven to 190°C/170°C/Gas Mark 5.

2 Place a paper muffin case in each hole in the muffin tray.

3 Gently mix together all the ingredients in the mixing bowl with the wooden spoon.

4 Using the dessert spoon, fill the muffin cases to the top.

5 Bake for 20–25 minutes.

6 Ask an adult to help you get them out of the oven and test them with a skewer to see if they are cooked. The skewer should come out clean.

7 Leave to cool while you make the icing – although these are delicious without icing, and a lot healthier, too!

8 If you want to add icing, place all the ingredients in a food processor and mix until you have a smooth, creamy mixture. Wait until the muffins are cool before icing them.

If you can find some Halloween cake decorations in the shops, put them on top of the muffins to serve at your Halloween party!

# SEASONAL EATING

October is apple season! Here are five fruity facts about apples:

1. Humans have been eating apples from as long ago as 6,500 BCE!

2. The average person eats 65 apples a year.

3. The science of apple-growing is known as 'pomology'.

4. Apples contain a chemical called 'boron' that increases brain activity.

5. It is said that it was an apple falling from a tree which led Sir Isaac Newton to understand how gravity works!

# GET PLANTING FOR SPRING

It might seem as though everything in the garden is dying away, but October is actually the perfect time to plant bulbs for next spring. You can plant daffodils, snowdrops, hyacinths, lilies and crocuses. Most of these like a place that will be warm and sunny come the spring time. You can plant them in pots or flowerbeds.

# THE DARK IS RISING

The days are getting shorter and shorter. However, we still have light evenings until the clocks change on Sunday 27th October. This means we get an extra hour in bed the night before. It can be confusing if you are a baby or an animal as it messes around with your mealtimes!

## Why Do the Clocks Change?

We didn't always bother with changing the clocks. In the old days, people went to bed when the sun went down and got up again when it rose. Midday was several minutes earlier in the east of the country than it was in the south, and several minutes later in the west. This meant that town clocks across the British Isles showed different times. The building of the railway network changed all that because the time had to be the same all over the country, or people would not have the faintest idea when to catch a train.

Then a man called William Willett suggested to parliament that if the clocks changed, we would all enjoy more daylight in the autumn and winter months. So, since 1916, the clocks go back one hour in October to 'save daylight' and in March the clocks are put forward to the original time. This is known as 'Daylight Saving'.

**TOP TIP**
In spring, the clocks spring forward an hour, and in the autumn, they fall back.

# THE MIGRATION OF BEWICK'S SWANS

Bewick's swans are among many birds and animals that follow nature's clock. They spend April–September in an area of northern Russia called the Russian tundra, where they breed. Then, in October, to escape the fierce cold weather in the north, they begin a long journey, migrating south-west. Many of them find their way to Britain and stay here until March when they begin their journey back to Russia. They arrive in their greatest numbers in the east of England, but can also be seen in the Severn estuary near Bristol in the west and also in Lancashire and Ireland.

## DID YOU KNOW...

Sadly, there are fewer Bewick's swans than there used to be. In 1995, it was thought that about 29,000 of the birds came to Europe. In recent years the number has dropped to around 18,000 and the numbers are believed to still be going down.

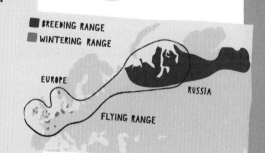

- BREEDING RANGE
- WINTERING RANGE

EUROPE

RUSSIA

FLYING RANGE

## Top Four Facts About Bewick's Swans

1 These amazing birds can live for 30 years.

2 They tend to stay with one partner until one of them dies. Some have stayed together for up to 21 years.

3 Bewick's swans often return to the same wetland area every year.

4 The babies, called cygnets, stay with their parents for the whole of their first winter and their parents guide them on their first migration so that they know where to go.

# TIME FOR BED

As well as birds and animals migrating, autumn is a time for some of them to hibernate, which means they go to sleep for the whole winter. There are not many creatures that do this in Britain, as our winters are not as cold as in other parts of the world.

**Why Do Animals Hibernate?**

It's not just because they like being warm and cosy – or lazy! Animals who hibernate aren't simply going to sleep – their bodies have adapted to make sure that they survive during the winter months. When they go into hibernation, their bodies slow right down so that they breathe more slowly, their hearts beat much more slowly and the temperature of their bodies drops. This means that they don't need to eat so much because their bodies are not using as much energy as when they are awake and running around. However, before they hibernate they make sure they eat lots and lots to fatten up so that they have plenty of energy in reserve during their long sleep.

# BRITISH ANIMALS THAT HIBERNATE

There are only three types of mammal that go into hibernation in this country. They are: hedgehogs, dormice and bats.

Some insects also hibernate, such as mason bees, queen bumblebees and butterflies.

Hedgehog

Bats

Frogs and toads slow down and sleep a lot more in the winter, but they don't actually hibernate – they still wake up occasionally to find food.

Dormouse

## Going into His Shell

Tortoises are also hibernating animals. Of course, you don't see them in the wild in this country because they come from warmer places such as Eastern Europe, Africa, South America and Asia. However, they are becoming very popular pets in Britain. If you would like to have a tortoise as a pet, you need to know how to put it into hibernation and how to look after it during these months. It is not as simple as putting them into a box and letting them get on with it!

First of all, you need to be sure that the tortoise is old enough, weighs enough and is in good enough health to be able to survive hibernation. If in doubt, talk to your local vet. You can also get very good advice from **www.tortoisecentre.co.uk**

## Be Warned!

Tortoises are very good at escaping! Even when you think you have tucked yours up safely for hibernation, he or she can find his way out of the box, so make sure you put your pet in a secure place so that you won't be hunting high and low for an escaped tortoise!

# November

## SPECIAL DAYS

**1st**   All Saints' Day (Christian celebration)

**2nd**   All Souls' Day (Christian celebration)

**5th**   Guy Fawkes Night (Bonfire Night)

**10th**   Prophet's Birthday (Muslim celebration)/
Remembrance Sunday

**11th**   Armistice Day (Remembrance Day)/Martinmas

**24th**   Stir-up Sunday (last Sunday before Advent)

**30th**   St Andrew's Day (Scotland)

# ANNIVERSARIES

**100 years ago . . .**

On 28 November 1919, Lady Astor was elected as a Member of Parliament and became the first woman to sit in the House of Commons.

**100 years ago . . .**

On the evening of 10 November 1919, King George V hosted a banquet in honour of the first Armistice Day (Remembrance Day) to remember those who had died in the First World War.

> *"So dull and dark are the November days.*
> *The lazy mist high up the evening curled,*
> *and now the morn quite hides in smoke and haze."*

JOHN CLARE (1793–1864)

We can no longer deny it – winter is on its way! The shortest day is less than two months' away, so it is no wonder that so many festivals this month celebrate light. Many festivals also focus on sweet-tasting food – a sweet treat can be just what you need when you've been outside, battling the cold! This is the time of year to tidy away the garden for winter, and a bonfire is a great way to get rid of dead leaves and wood.

## Why is November Called November?

The word November comes from the Latin word for the number nine, *novem*. This is because, just like September and October before it, November keeps its name from a time when the calendar had only ten months.

The Anglo-Saxons called this month *Blotmonath,* which means 'blood month'. This is because it was traditional at this time of year to kill farm animals and preserve the meat for the winter months ahead.

## Constellation of the Month

*Taurus* is the Latin word for 'bull'. Look out for this constellation in the east, where it starts the night low in the sky. If you look for the bright orange giant star called Aldebaran, that will help you find the rest of the constellation.

## November Birth Signs

People born under the sign of Scorpio
(the scorpion) on or between 23rd October and
21st November are said to be brave, passionate,
stubborn and a true friend. They like the truth,
facts and being right! They also like to have deep,
long-lasting friendships.

Sagittarius is represented by a centaur – a mythological
creature who is half-man, half-horse. People born
under the sign of Sagittarius, on or between 22nd
November and 21st December, are supposed to be
generous and have a great sense of humour.
They can also be very impatient and will
often speak first and think after!

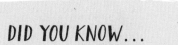

## DID YOU KNOW...

The birth signs are divided into the four elements of nature:
earth, air, fire and water.

### *Earth* Taurus, Virgo, Capricorn
These signs represent people who are realistic and loyal and
who will stick with their family and friends through hard times.

### *Air* Gemini, Libra, Aquarius
People born under these signs are friendly and communicative
and enjoy giving advice.

### *Fire* Aries, Leo and Sagittarius
People born under these signs might get angry quickly, but
they will also forgive easily. They are adventurers who are
always ready for action.

### *Water* Cancer, Scorpio and Pisces
These signs are linked to people who love deep conversations
and close friendships.

# FESTIVAL FUN

**5th November** *Guy Fawkes or Bonfire Night*

## "Remember, remember the 5ᵗʰ of November Gunpowder, treason and plot!"

This is an annual commemoration of the day in 1605 when a man called Guy Fawkes was arrested for being a member of the 'Gunpowder Plot'. The plot was made up of a group of men who wanted to blow up King James I and the Houses of Parliament in London. Guy Fawkes was found hiding beneath the House of Lords, guarding some explosives. Thankfully, the bombs never went off.

Nowadays people spend the evening going to firework displays, standing around a big bonfire and eating hot dogs! It is a great way to chase away the winter blues.

**10th November** *Prophet's Birthday*

In the UK and all over the world, some Muslims see this as a day to celebrate. In some countries there are street parades, the mosques are decorated and children read out poems about the Prophet's life. People can spend the day donating food and money to charity, too. Other Muslims see this day as a time for concentrating on the holy book, the *Qur'an*.

## 11th November *Armistice Day (Remembrance Day)*

Before the First World War, this day was originally known as Martinmas or St Martin's Day. St Martin is the patron saint of the poor. The day was spent celebrating the change of seasons and getting ready for winter. Big feasts were held, and people traditionally ate goose, beef, black pudding (a kind of blood sausage) and haggis (sheep's stomach stuffed with chopped sheep's heart, lungs, liver, herbs and oats).

Since 1918, 11th November has become better known as Armistice Day or Remembrance Day. It is a time for remembering all those who were killed in the First and Second World War and other wars that have since followed.

In 1919, the first two-minute silence was held to remember the dead. In 1939, this two-minute silence was moved to the Sunday nearest to 11th November so that it did not interfere with people's work. People traditionally wear a red poppy around this time to show that they have not forgotten the people who died in the war.

## 24th November *Stir-Up Sunday*

This is the last Sunday before Advent, which is the period of time in which Christians prepare for Christmas, and is the day people traditionally make their Christmas puddings. In the old days, it was a time for families to get together to mix and steam the pudding. Everyone would take a turn to stir the pudding and make a special wish for the year ahead.

In some houses, silver coins are added to the pudding mix as finding a coin on Christmas Day is supposed to bring good luck.

### DID YOU KNOW...

Traditionally, the pudding is stirred from east to west in honour of the Three Wise Men who came from the east to visit the baby Jesus.

# REMEMBER, REMEMBER... HEDGEHOGS

★ If you are having a bonfire for Bonfire Night, it is best to pile up the leaves and wood on the day of the actual bonfire. If you do it too far in advance, a hedgehog might think you have made a lovely place in which it can hibernate.

★ You can stop hedgehogs from finding their way into a bonfire pile by building a small fence with chicken wire around the edge. The wire should be about one metre high and should be held in place with bamboo sticks. Try to make the wire slope outwards – this will stop the hedgehogs from trying to climb in.

★ If you have already helped make a nice mound of garden waste to burn, perhaps you could move it to another place for the actual bonfire? This will give you a chance to look through the leaves and so on to make sure that there are no hedgehogs hiding inside the pile.

★ Just in case you have missed a hedgehog, make sure the adult in charge of the bonfire lights the pile on one side only and keep away from the unlit side. That way, any hiding hedgehogs have a chance of escaping to safety.

★ Finally, if you do find a hedgehog, put on some gardening gloves (or oven gloves) before touching its spiky little body. This is also to protect the hedgehog as they don't like getting the smell of humans on them!

★ Then, when you scoop up the creature, make sure you pick it up along with any leaves or bedding it has pulled around itself. Hedgehogs make cosy little nests, and you don't want to undo all their hard work.

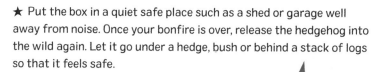

★ Put the hedgehog, with its nest, in a high-sided cardboard box with plenty of newspaper or old towels. You'll need to put a lid on too – remember to make some air holes in the lid so that the hedgehog can breathe.

★ Put the box in a quiet safe place such as a shed or garage well away from noise. Once your bonfire is over, release the hedgehog into the wild again. Let it go under a hedge, bush or behind a stack of logs so that it feels safe.

## DID YOU KNOW...

The number of hedgehogs in Britain is falling fast. To find out more about how to help hedgehogs, visit **www.britishhedgehogs.org.uk**

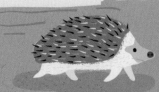

# STARS OF THE EVENING

Have you ever been out for a walk, or on a long car journey, and seen a black mass of birds swooping and circling in the sky? If so, you have probably seen a 'murmuration' of starlings. It is the most amazing sight – like a swirling black cloud of birds that is constantly on the move. The birds perform incredible acrobatic stunts and the flock makes breath-taking patterns in the sky.

Murmurations become more common in November. More and more birds will flock together as the month goes on. Starlings choose places to roost together that are well sheltered from bad weather and predators. This means that they like woodlands, reed beds, cliffs and even disused buildings, too.

There are some beautiful reserves in Britain that have fantastic spots for watching murmurations: Gretna Green in Scotland and Brighton Pier are two of the more famous ones.

## DID YOU KNOW...

The number of starlings roosting in one place can grow to as many as 750,000! They group together for safety, as predators such as hawks and peregrine falcons find it much harder to hunt down one bird in the middle of the huge hypnotising flocks. They also come together to keep warm at night and possibly to 'talk' to each other about where the best feeding areas are!

# SEE THE SEALS

Grey seal

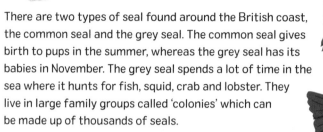

There are two types of seal found around the British coast, the common seal and the grey seal. The common seal gives birth to pups in the summer, whereas the grey seal has its babies in November. The grey seal spends a lot of time in the sea where it hunts for fish, squid, crab and lobster. They live in large family groups called 'colonies' which can be made up of thousands of seals.

The grey seal prefers the colder water found in the north of the country and is most likely to be seen off the coast of Northumberland, Lincolnshire and the Orkney Islands.

The grey seal grows to a much larger size than the common seal and males are much bigger than females.

The main difference between the common seal and the grey seal is that the grey seal has a much longer nose or 'snout' than the common seal and has nostrils spaced further apart!

Seals like to leave the water to rest and bask in the sun after they have been hunting.

The females care for their young for a few weeks until the soft white fur of the babies has been replaced with the adult's waterproof coat!

Numbers of grey seals are increasing all over the world.

Common seal

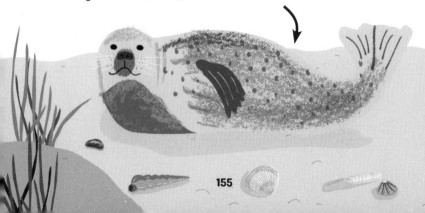

# LET'S GO FLY A KITE

It can get quite windy in November – which means it's perfect weather for flying a kite! You don't need to spend money on an expensive one. Have a go at making your own recyclable kite from newspaper and wood.

**You will need:**

Newspaper
5 m string
Sticks about 60 cm long
Glue (a bottle with a nozzle for easy spreading is good)
1 m coloured ribbon

**TOP TIP**
Make the kite on a rainy day – then wait for a bright, dry, windy day to try it out.

1. *Look for sticks in the park, garden or woods.*

2. *Use small pieces of string to tie the sticks into a cross – the horizontal stick will need to be slightly shorter than the vertical one.*

3. *Tie the string around the edge of the sticks to make a diamond shape. Don't cut the string until you have done this! (You might need to ask an adult to make small cuts or notches into the sticks to help the string stay in place.)*

4. *Unfold your newspaper and cut a pattern to match the shape of your kite frame. Make sure the paper is about 3–5 cm larger than your frame all the way around so that you can fold the edges over the string.*

5 On a flat surface, lay out your paper with your stick and string frame on top, then fold the edges of your paper over the string.

6 Glue the paper into place.

7 Tie the longest piece of string you have to where the sticks cross. This is the string you'll hold on to when you fly your kite, so the longer the string, the higher the kite will fly!

8 To decorate your kite, tie a long ribbon (or ribbons!) to the longest point of the diamond. This is the tail of your kite.

9 Run outside on a windy day, take hold of the long string, run a little more, and . . . your kite will soar up into the sky like a paper bird!

# MAKING MINCEMEAT

This is a great indoor activity for those dark, wet November days. Jars of homemade mincemeat make a lovely gift, and will keep for up to three years, so it is worth making the full quantity, even if it's so tasty you don't want to give it away!

## DID YOU KNOW...

Mincemeat used to contain chunks of actual meat mixed in with the fruit! Nowadays recipes use suet, which is an animal fat. However, you can use vegetable suet instead.

## TOP TIP

If you don't like candied peel you can use chopped dried apricots instead.

**You will need:**

Large oven-proof mixing bowl
Wooden spoon
Clean cloth (tea towel or muslin)
6 x 350 ml sterilised glass jars
Greaseproof paper
Scissors
Foil

450 g Bramley apples, cored and chopped into small pieces
50 g chopped almonds
4 teaspoons of mixed spice
½ teaspoon of ground cinnamon
¼ teaspoon of freshly grated nutmeg
225 g shredded suet (original or vegetarian)
350 g raisins
225 g sultanas
225 g currants
225 g candied peel, chopped into small pieces
350 g soft dark brown sugar
Grated zest and juice of 3 oranges
Grated zest and juice of 3 lemons

1 Pour all the ingredients into a large mixing bowl and give them a good stir.

2 Cover the bowl with a clean cloth and leave in a cool place overnight. This allows the flavours to deepen and become more delicious.

3 The next day, preheat the oven to 110°C/90°C fan/Gas Mark ¼.

4 Remove the cloth and cover the bowl loosely with foil.

5 Place the bowl in the oven for 3 hours, then remove it and allow it to cool, stirring occasionally. (Don't worry if it looks fatty and gloopy! It will change as it cools.)

6 When the mincemeat is cold, stir it again, then fill the sterilised glass jars to the top.

7 Cut out circles of greaseproof paper to put on top of the mincemeat before fitting the lids.

Decorate the jars with hand-drawn labels and colourful ribbon if you want to give them away as gifts. You can also cut out a circle of fabric or shiny paper to cover the lids to make the jars look extra special.

**TOP TIP**
To sterilise glass jars, wash and dry them, then place them on a baking tray in the oven at 180°C/ 160°C fan/Gas Mark 4 for 5 minutes.

# December

## SPECIAL DAYS

**1st**   First Sunday of Advent (Christian celebration)

**21st**   Winter solstice/Midwinter/ Yule (pagan celebration)/Start of winter

**22nd**   First day of Hanukkah (Jewish celebration)

**24th**   Christmas Eve/First day of Christmas

**25th**   Christmas Day (Christian celebration)

**26th**   Boxing Day

**30th**   Last day of Hanukkah

**31st**   New Year's Eve/Hogmanay

# ANNIVERSARIES

**100 years ago . . .**

On 10 December 1919, Sir Ross Macpherson Smith and his brother, Keith Smith, were the first men to fly from London to Australia. They took off from Hounslow Heath Aerodrome on 12th November and did the flight in stages so that it took 28 days. Now you can fly non-stop from London to Australia in around 17 hours!

> ## "Chill December brings the sleet, Blazing fire and Christmas treat."

SARA COLERIDGE (1802–1852)

In Britain, Christmas has become the main focus of this month. It is not the only festival going on, though. There are lots of other celebrations of light during this month because it contains the shortest day of the year. For many thousands of years people have spent dark December thinking ahead to a time when the sun will come back. Whichever festival you celebrate, you are bound to have lots of fun, food and treats!

## Why is December Called December?

This month gets its name from the Latin word for tenth, *decem*. The Anglo-Saxons called December *Ærra Geola* or the month 'before Yule'. Yule was an important winter festival and is still celebrated today by pagans. Many of the 'Yuletide' traditions have found their way into things we now think of as Christmas traditions.

### Phases of the Moon in December 2019

| First Quarter | Full Moon | Last Quarter | New Moon |
|---|---|---|---|
| 4th December | 12th December | 19th December | 26th December |

The full moon this month is known as the Cold Moon or Long Night Moon.

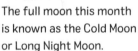

# WHATEVER THE WEATHER

December may be the start of winter, but by the end of the month the days are already getting lighter. It is because of this promise of longer, lighter days that the longest night has traditionally been a time for celebration. The dark can be sad or scary sometimes, but just think: if there was no darkness, there would be no light! This is what all the festivals this month are about: finding light in the darkness. The one thing you may hope for and not get this month is snow. You are far more likely to get snow from February through to March in Britain.

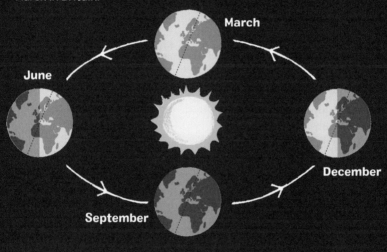

## DID YOU KNOW...

Contrary to what people often think, the seasons don't change because of how far the Earth is from the sun. The change happens because the Earth goes around the sun at a tilted angle of about 23.4°. This causes different amounts of sunlight to reach the northern and southern hemispheres throughout the year. In fact, the Earth is closest to the sun a few weeks after the winter solstice.

# FESTIVAL FUN

There's so much festival fun this month, you could be forgiven for thinking that December is one long celebration from start to finish!

## 1st December *First Sunday of Advent*

Advent lasts for four Sundays leading up to Christmas. Advent always begins on the Sunday that falls between 27th November and 3rd December. In churches, Christians light one candle every Sunday of Advent. It is common for people to also begin their own countdown to Christmas on 1st December with Advent calendars or Advent candles which have the numbers 1 to 24 on them.

## 21st December *Winter solstice or Midwinter or Yule*

The winter solstice or Midwinter falls on the shortest day of the year and has been celebrated in Britain for hundreds of years. Many pagan traditions of Yule have found their way into the celebration of Christmas. At Yule, pagans light candles and fires, decorate their homes with evergreen plants, feast, dance, and give gifts. All these things are now traditional at Christmas, too.

Pagans also believe that hanging a sprig of holly near the door brings good luck and keeps away evil spirits. Mistletoe is also hung as a decoration and as a blessing and symbol of new life.

# THE YULE LOG

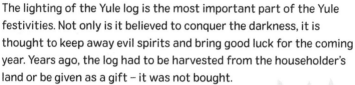

The lighting of the Yule log is the most important part of the Yule festivities. Not only is it believed to conquer the darkness, it is thought to keep away evil spirits and bring good luck for the coming year. Years ago, the log had to be harvested from the householder's land or be given as a gift – it was not bought.

The Yule log would be placed in the fireplace and decorated with evergreen leaves, before cider or ale was poured on it and it was dusted with flour. Then it was lit with a piece of Yule log from the year before and the log would burn for 12 days. Then it was put out and a piece saved for the following year.

**Five Ways to** *Celebrate Midwinter*

★ Go on a walk to gather greenery for your home.
★ Light a fire or a circle of candles.
★ Tell stories around the fire or by candlelight.
★ Have a feast with your favourite food and favourite family and friends!
★ Write down a list of everything you have to be thankful for in the past year.

**22nd–30th December** *Hanukkah*

Sometimes spelled *Chanukah*, this Jewish festival lasts for eight days. During this time, Jewish people remember how the Second Temple in Jerusalem was dedicated to God. Hanukkah is often called the Festival of Lights because the holiday is celebrated with the lighting of the *menorah* candlestick. Traditional foods are served such as potato pancakes and jam-filled doughnuts called *sufganiyot*.

# STAR-TOPPED MINCE PIES

**You will need:**

Sieve
Food processor
Shallow freezer-proof bowl
or dish
Rolling pin
2 x 12 cm holed tart trays,
greased with a little butter
5.5 cm circular biscuit
cutter with fluted edges
4 cm star-shaped biscuit
cutter

240 g plain flour
120 g cold butter, cut into small
pieces
Juice of one orange mixed with
a pinch of salt
350 g Christmas mincemeat
Teaspoon
Icing sugar for
dusting

## TOP TIP

This recipe makes 24 pies.
They can be kept in an
air-tight container for
a week and reheated
before serving.

1 Preheat the oven to 220°C/200°C fan/
Gas Mark 7.
2 Sieve the flour into a freezer-proof
bowl or dish and add the butter. Gently mix.
3 Place the dish in the freezer for 10 minutes.
4 Take the dish out of the freezer and tip the
contents into the food processor.
5 Blend the flour and butter until the mixture looks
like breadcrumbs.
6 Very slowly, add the orange juice and salt through the funnel of
the machine. Stop adding the juice just before you see the crumbs turn
into a complete ball of dough. You may not need to use all the juice!
7 If you run out of juice and the mixture is still crumbly, add
some very cold water, drop by drop, until the mixture becomes
more like dough.
8 Take the dough out and wrap it in greaseproof paper, then
pop it in the fridge for 20 minutes.
9 Tip some flour on to a work surface. Divide the dough into two
balls. Take one ball and roll it out until it is about 2 mm thick.
10 Use the circular biscuit cutter to cut out 24 circles
and press them gently into the greased tart trays.

11 *Fill each tart with about 2 teaspoons of mincemeat.*

12 *Use the star-shaped biscuit cutter to cut out 24 stars and put one on each pie.*

13 *Ask an adult to help you put the pies in the oven and set a timer for about 10–15 minutes. You'll need to check on the pies after 10 minutes as they don't take long to cook.*

14 *Take the trays out of the oven and gently remove the pies, then put them on a wire rack to cool.*

15 *Dust with icing sugar before serving.*

## Make a *Yule Log*

There are quite a few people who don't much like the taste of mince pies or Christmas pudding. If you're one of them, why not try making a Yule Log? You could buy a chocolate Swiss roll and decorate it with chocolate butter icing and then dust it with icing sugar to make it look like a log covered in snow!

## 25th December *Christmas*

The word Christmas comes from the Anglo-Saxon word *Cristesmæsse*. It is the Christian celebration of the birth of Jesus Christ. In fact, his birth date is unknown. However, Christians wanted a day to celebrate their belief that Jesus brought goodness and light into the world. As there were already 'light festivals' at this time of year such as Yule, it made sense to have Christmas then as well.

Saturnalia is an ancient Roman festival that probably influenced how and when Christmas is celebrated. It was dedicated to the god Saturn. All work and business stopped during the festival, and slaves were given a few days of freedom. People said *"io Saturnalia"* to each other the way people today might say "Happy Christmas!" or "Happy Hanukkah!" At the end of the festival people would make presents of candles to one another or wax models of fruit.

## 31st December *New Year's Eve or Hogmanay*

It is the last day of the year! Just before midnight it is traditional to turn on a radio or television to see the countdown of the last few minutes of the old year and to watch the display of fireworks over the River Thames in London. At this point, people often hug and kiss and start to sing the song 'Auld Lang Syne' – although they often don't know the words! Here they are so that you can sing them this year:

"Should auld acquaintance be forgot
and never brought to mind?
Should auld acquaintance be forgot,
and auld lang syne?
For auld lang syne my dear,
For auld lang syne,
We'll tak' a cup o' kindness yet,
for auld lang syne."

The words were written by the Scottish poet Robert Burns in 1788. The song asks if it's right to forget old friends and things that have happened in the past.

### Just After Midnight...

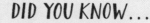

In Scotland, New Year's Eve is known as Hogmanay. If you're lucky enough to be in Scotland on 1st January (and you're allowed to stay up on New Year's Eve until after

## DID YOU KNOW...

*Auld Lang Syne* means 'long, long ago' or 'days gone by'. In the song it means 'for the sake of old times'.

midnight!), you might be able to join in with the tradition of First Footing on January 1st.

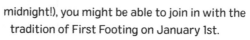

The 'first foot' to come in through the front door after the last stroke of midnight is supposed to bring good luck. The 'first footer' should be carrying a piece of coal, some bread, salt and a small drink (known as a 'wee dram'). These items are thought to bring warmth, good food, long-life and good cheer for the year ahead.

# 'STAINED GLASS' BISCUIT DECORATIONS

These can be hung on a Christmas tree or strung up on string to decorate the house for Hanukkah or Yule. Or you can give them as presents!

**You will need:**

Baking tray
Greaseproof paper
Biscuit cutters (such as stars, hearts, holly leaves or Christmas trees)
Electric hand whisk
Large bowl
Sieve
Wooden spoon
Rolling pin
Small blunt knife
Metal skewer
Ribbon or string
Wire rack

150 g butter (softened)
100 g muscovado sugar
1 large egg
250 g plain flour plus more for dusting
1 tsp baking powder
pinch salt
1 tablespoon of mixed spice
1 teaspoon of vanilla extract
1 pack of boiled sweets (red, green and yellow work best)

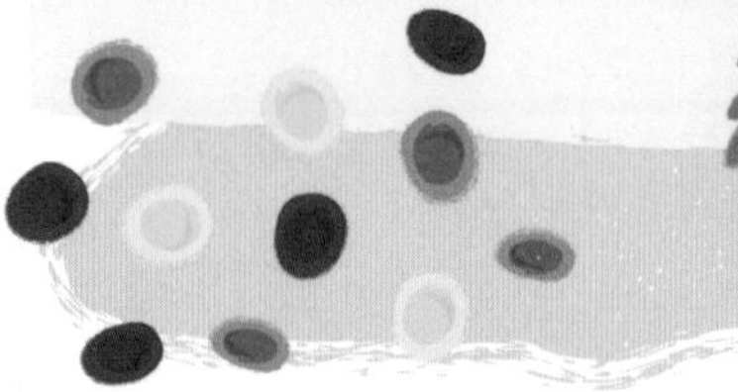

1. Preheat the oven to 180°C/160°C fan/Gas Mark 4 and line a baking tray with greaseproof paper.

2. In a large bowl, whisk together the butter and sugar. When the mixture looks light and creamy, add the egg and mix thoroughly.

3. Sieve the flour, baking powder, salt, and mixed spice together and add to the creamy mixture.

4. Add the vanilla extract and mix with a wooden spoon until the mixture looks like dough.

5. Turn the dough on to a work surface sprinkled with flour.

6. Roll the dough to about 1 cm thickness.

7. Use the biscuit cutters to cut out shapes and place them on to the lined baking tray (you may need more than one tray, or to cook in batches).

8. Using a smaller cutter or a small blunt knife cut out the centre of each biscuit.

9. Place a boiled sweet into the hole (cut the sweet in half if your hole is smaller than 2.5 cm).

10. Place the tray in the preheated oven and cook the biscuits for 15 minutes, or until they are golden-brown and crisp and the sweet has melted.

11. As soon as the biscuits are baked and while they are still warm, use the metal skewer to poke a hole out of the top of each biscuit. Be careful not to make this hole too near the edge of the biscuit. Once the melted sweets have hardened, transfer them to a wire rack to cool.

12. Thread a length of string or ribbon through the hole and hang the biscuits up so that light can shine through the centres like stained glass.

# OUT IN THE WILD

While we humans are busy huddling by the fire and staying warm and cosy, nature carries on working. If you have had enough of being stuck indoors, get your family out on a nature walk. Wrap up warm and keep your eyes peeled. It might be winter, but there's still lots to see!

Robins are very busy at this time of year singing to protect their territories and finding food.

Listen out as the sun goes down and you might hear tawny owls calling to one another. The female calls out "too-wit" and the male answers her, "too-whoo!"

Go for a walk around a river estuary. Birds flock to these places in the winter as the water does not freeze so there is always a lot of food to be found. You might even see a kingfisher or an otter.

Foxes are out hunting in the early evening. They can often be seen slinking into hedges or scurrying down driveways just after the sun has set.

Go for a walk by the sea. This is a great time of year to search the empty beaches for treasures – strange twisted lumps of driftwood, shells, pebbles and seed pods can all be used to make beautiful decorations.

Walk in the woods too! Collect holly and ivy and pine cones and twigs and then come home and have fun making natural decorations for the house.

# PINE CONE SANTAS

These make lovely decorations or presents, or you could sell them at your school fair to make money for charity.

**You will need:**

**Lots of small pine cones**
**Red paper**
**Scissors**
**Cotton wool**
**Packet of small 'googly' eyes**
**Strong paper glue or a glue gun**
**Loo roll tube**

★ Gather some pine cones while you are out on a winter walk.
★ Let them dry out in the airing cupboard or in a warm dry place.
★ Make hats by drawing around the end of an empty loo roll tube on the paper.
★ Cut out the circle and cut a slit into the centre.
★ Bend the circle to form a cone and glue the slit to fix the cone in place.
★ Glue on the hat, plus some googly eyes and cotton wool for a beard.

# WRAPPING UP THE YEAR

*"There is a time for everything, and a season for every activity under the heavens."*

(ECCLESIASTES 3, FOUND IN THE HEBREW *TANAKH* AND THE *BIBLE*)

So, it's time to say goodbye to the old and make way for the new. Maybe you'll make those new year's resolutions all over again . . . and just maybe you'll do better at keeping them in 2020! Whatever you do, and wherever you are, thank you for reading this book and

## HAPPY NEW YEAR TO YOU AND YOUR FRIENDS AND FAMILY!

# CALENDAR 2019

## January

| Mo | Tu | We | Th | Fr | Sa | Su |
|----|----|----|----|----|----|----|
|    | 1  | 2  | 3  | 4  | 5  | 6  |
| 7  | 8  | 9  | 10 | 11 | 12 | 13 |
| 14 | 15 | 16 | 17 | 18 | 19 | 20 |
| 21 | 22 | 23 | 24 | 25 | 26 | 27 |
| 28 | 29 | 30 | 31 |    |    |    |

**Phases of the Moon**

6: ● 14: ◐ 21: ○ 27: ◑

## February

| Mo | Tu | We | Th | Fr | Sa | Su |
|----|----|----|----|----|----|----|
|    |    |    |    | 1  | 2  | 3  |
| 4  | 5  | 6  | 7  | 8  | 9  | 10 |
| 11 | 12 | 13 | 14 | 15 | 16 | 17 |
| 18 | 19 | 20 | 21 | 22 | 23 | 24 |
| 25 | 26 | 27 | 28 |    |    |    |

**Phases of the Moon**

4: ● 12: ◐ 19: ○ 26: ◑

# March

| Mo | Tu | We | Th | Fr | Sa | Su |
|----|----|----|----|----|----|----|
|    |    |    |    | 1  | 2  | 3  |
| 4  | 5  | 6  | 7  | 8  | 9  | 10 |
| 11 | 12 | 13 | 14 | 15 | 16 | 17 |
| 18 | 19 | 20 | 21 | 22 | 23 | 24 |
| 25 | 26 | 27 | 28 | 29 | 30 | 31 |

**Phases of the Moon**

6: ● 14: ◐ 21: ○ 28: ◑

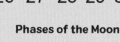

# April

| Mo | Tu | We | Th | Fr | Sa | Su |
|----|----|----|----|----|----|----|
| 1  | 2  | 3  | 4  | 5  | 6  | 7  |
| 8  | 9  | 10 | 11 | 12 | 13 | 14 |
| 15 | 16 | 17 | 18 | 19 | 20 | 21 |
| 22 | 23 | 24 | 25 | 26 | 27 | 28 |
| 29 | 30 |    |    |    |    |    |

**Phases of the Moon**

5: ● 12: ◐ 19: ○ 26: ◑

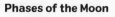

# May

| Mo | Tu | We | Th | Fr | Sa | Su |
|----|----|----|----|----|----|----|
|    |    | 1  | 2  | 3  | 4  | 5  |
| 6  | 7  | 8  | 9  | 10 | 11 | 12 |
| 13 | 14 | 15 | 16 | 17 | 18 | 19 |
| 20 | 21 | 22 | 23 | 24 | 25 | 26 |
| 27 | 28 | 29 | 30 | 31 |    |    |

**Phases of the Moon**

4: ● 12: ◑ 18: ○ 26: ◑

# June

| Mo | Tu | We | Th | Fr | Sa | Su |
|----|----|----|----|----|----|----|
|    |    |    |    |    | 1  | 2  |
| 3  | 4  | 5  | 6  | 7  | 8  | 9  |
| 10 | 11 | 12 | 13 | 14 | 15 | 16 |
| 17 | 18 | 19 | 20 | 21 | 22 | 23 |
| 24 | 25 | 26 | 27 | 28 | 29 | 30 |

**Phases of the Moon**

3: ● 10: ◑ 17: ◔ 25: ◑

# July

| Mo | Tu | We | Th | Fr | Sa | Su |
|----|----|----|----|----|----|----|
| 1 | 2 | 3 | 4 | 5 | 6 | 7 |
| 8 | 9 | 10 | 11 | 12 | 13 | 14 |
| 15 | 16 | 17 | 18 | 19 | 20 | 21 |
| 22 | 23 | 24 | 25 | 26 | 27 | 28 |
| 29 | 30 | 31 | | | | |

**Phases of the Moon**

2: ●    9: ◑    16: ○    25: ◑

# August

| Mo | Tu | We | Th | Fr | Sa | Su |
|----|----|----|----|----|----|----|
| | | | 1 | 2 | 3 | 4 |
| 5 | 6 | 7 | 8 | 9 | 10 | 11 |
| 12 | 13 | 14 | 15 | 16 | 17 | 18 |
| 19 | 20 | 21 | 22 | 23 | 24 | 25 |
| 26 | 27 | 28 | 29 | 30 | 31 | |

**Phases of the Moon**

1: ●    7: ◑    15: ○    23: ◑    30: ●

# September

| Mo | Tu | We | Th | Fr | Sa | Su |
|----|----|----|----|----|----|----|
|    |    |    |    |    |    | 1  |
| 2  | 3  | 4  | 5  | 6  | 7  | 8  |
| 9  | 10 | 11 | 12 | 13 | 14 | 15 |
| 16 | 17 | 18 | 19 | 20 | 21 | 22 |
| 23 | 24 | 25 | 26 | 27 | 28 | 29 |
| 30 |    |    |    |    |    |    |

**Phases of the Moon**

6: ◑   14: ◔   22: ◐   28: ●

# October

| Mo | Tu | We | Th | Fr | Sa | Su |
|----|----|----|----|----|----|----|
|    | 1  | 2  | 3  | 4  | 5  | 6  |
| 7  | 8  | 9  | 10 | 11 | 12 | 13 |
| 14 | 15 | 16 | 17 | 18 | 19 | 20 |
| 21 | 22 | 23 | 24 | 25 | 26 | 27 |
| 28 | 29 | 30 | 31 |    |    |    |

**Phases of the Moon**

5: ◑   13: ○   21: ◐   28: ●

# November

|Mo|Tu|We|Th|Fr|Sa|Su|
|---|---|---|---|---|---|---|
| | | | |1|2|3|
|4|5|6|7|8|9|10|
|11|12|13|14|15|16|17|
|18|19|20|21|22|23|24|
|25|26|27|28|29|30| |

**Phases of the Moon**

4: 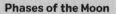 12: 19: 26:

# December

|Mo|Tu|We|Th|Fr|Sa|Su|
|---|---|---|---|---|---|---|
| | | | | | |1|
|2|3|4|5|6|7|8|
|9|10|11|12|13|14|15|
|16|17|18|19|20|21|22|
|23|24|25|26|27|28|29|
|30|31| | | | | |

**Phases of the Moon**

4: 12: 19: 26:

# NOTES

182

183

# GLOSSARY

**Advent** The period leading up to Christmas

**All Saints' Eve** A Christian festival to remember saints and loved ones who have died

**Allah** The name of God for Muslims and Arab Christians

**Anglo-Saxons** People who lived in Great Britain from 410 until 1066

**Apple Day** A celebration of apples and orchards

**April Fool's Day** The first day of April, when people play jokes on each other

**Ascension Day** A Christian holy day to celebrate the day Jesus rose into heaven

**Ash Wednesday** The beginning of Lent

**Battle of the Boyne** (1690) A battle fought in Ireland, won by the Protestant King William of Orange against the Catholic King James II

**Beltane** An ancient pagan festival that celebrates the return of summer

**Bible** The Christian holy book

**Birthday Honours** The titles given to people on the Queen's official birthday

**Birth flower** A flower linked to the month of a person's birth

**Birthstone** A gemstone linked to the month of a person's birth

**Blue moon** A second full moon in a calendar month

**Buddhist** Someone who believes in and follows the teachings of the Buddha

**Burns Night** A celebration of the Scottish poet Robert Burns

**Candlemas** A Christian festival celebrating the first time that baby Jesus was taken to the temple

**Catholic** Someone who follows a branch of Christianity led by the Pope

**Chinese New Year** A colourful celebration of the start of the Chinese year, also known as the 'Spring Festival'

**Christian** Someone who follows the religion of Christianity and believes in God, Jesus Christ and the teachings of the *Bible*

**Church** The Christian place of worship

**Colony** A group of the same type of animals, insects or plants that live together

**Crop circle** A pattern made by flattening crops in a field, usually done overnight

**D-Day** The day that Allied forces invaded northern France during the Second World War

**Diwali** A Hindu festival of lights to celebrate the victory of light over darkness

**Easter** A Christian festival to remember the death and return to life of Jesus Christ

**Eid al-Adha** Also known as the 'Sacrifice Feast', this Islamic festival honours Ibrahim's willingness to obey Allah and marks the end of the *Hajj* pilgrimage to Mecca

**Eid al-Fitr** Also known as the 'Festival of the Breaking of the Fast', this Islamic festival is a three-day celebration to mark the end of Ramadan

**Equator** An imaginary line drawn around the middle of the Earth at an equal distance from the north and south poles

**Epiphany** A Christian holy day, held in January, which marks the end of the Christmas period

**Equinox** The time twice a year when the length of day and night is exactly equal

**Eta Aquarids** A meteor shower formed by particles of dust left behind by Halley's Comet

**Fast** To spend a period of time without eating or drinking

**Fertility** The ability to create children or young

**First Footing** A Scottish New Year's tradition, where the 'first footer' is the first person to walk through the door after midnight

**First quarter** One quarter of the way through the moon's cycle, when we can see exactly half of the moon at night

**Full moon** When the entire face of the moon is lit up by the sun's rays

**Ganesh Chaturthi** A 10-day Hindu festival to worship the god Ganesha

**Gemstone** A precious or semi-precious stone

**Gleaning** Gathering leftover grain after a harvest

**Guy Fawkes** A member of a group of English Catholics who tried to assassinate King James in 1604 by blowing up the Houses of Parliament

**Hanukkah** An eight-day 'festival of lights' celebrated by Jewish people, to remember how the Jewish army freed Jerusalem and took back the temple, which they re-dedicated to God

**Harvest** Gathering crops

**Hemisphere** Half of the Earth, divided into northern and southern hemispheres by the equator

**Hibernate** When an animal or plant goes to sleep for the winter

**Hindu** Someone who follows the South Asian religion of Hinduism, involving the belief in reincarnation and the worship of many gods

**Hogmanay** The Scottish word for the last day of the year

**Holi** A Hindu spring festival in celebration of the god Krishna

**Holy Spirit** Christians believe God exists in three forms at the same time, as God in heaven, as Jesus Christ in heaven, and as the Holy Spirit, which is everywhere

**Imbolc** A pagan festival marking the beginning of spring

**Isra and Mi'raj** An Islamic celebration of the Prophet Muhammad's journey from Mecca to Jerusalem and his journey into heaven, when Allah revealed to Muhammad that Muslims should pray five times a day

**Jain** Someone who follows the ancient Indian religion of Jainism that teaches *ahimsa* (non-violence) to all living creatures

**Jerusalem** The capital city of Israel, believed to be holy by Jews, Christians and Muslims

**Jew** Someone who follows the religion of Judaism and believes in God, the Hebrew prophets and the teachings of the *Torah*

**Lammas** A pagan celebration of the first harvest

**Last quarter** Three quarters of the way through the moon's cycle, when we can see exactly half of the moon at night

**Leap year** A year with 366 days in it, which occurs once every four years

**Lent** A Christian period of fasting in the run-up to Easter

**Litha** The Anglo-Saxon word for midsummer

**Lohri** A Punjabi midwinter festival celebrated by Sikhs and Hindus

**Lughnasadh** A Gaelic festival celebrating the beginning of the harvest season

**Maia** The Greek goddess of fertility

**Matzo** A flatbread that Jewish people eat at Passover

**May Day** The first day of May, celebrated by dancing and singing

**Mecca** The holiest city of Islam

**Meteor** A fiery streak in the sky, created when dust and rocks from the tail of a comet pass through the Earth's atmosphere

**Michaelmas** A Christian festival held at the end of September to honour the angels

**Midsummer** The longest day and the shortest night of the year, also known as the summer solstice

**Midwinter** The shortest day and the longest night of the year, also known as the winter solstice

**Migrate** To move from one place to another

**Morris dancing** A form of English folk dance with music

**Mosque** The Islamic place of worship

**Muhammad** The Muslim Prophet and founder of Islam

**Murmuration** When hundreds or thousands of starlings fly together in a flowing pattern

**Muslim** Someone who follows the religion of Islam and believes in Allah, the Prophet Muhammad, the five pillars of Islam and the teachings of the *Qur'an*

**Neap tide** A tide that happens twice a month, when the difference between high tide and low tide is at its lowest

**New moon** The first phase in the moon's cycle, when just a very thin crescent shape is visible at night

**Old Testament** The first part of the *Bible*, originally written in Hebrew

**Ostara** A pagan festival which is celebrated at the spring equinox

**Pagan** A follower of paganism, a pre-Christian religion, who believes in many gods and goddesses

**Passover** A Jewish celebration to remember how Moses helped the Israelites escape from Egypt

**Plaster of Paris** A mixture of powder and water, which dries quickly to make a plaster cast

**Pentecost** A Christian festival on the seventh Sunday after Easter, to celebrate the day after his death when Jesus returned to his disciples in the form of the Holy Spirit

**Promised Land** The land that Jewish people believe was given by God to Abraham and his descendants

**Purée** A thick liquid made from cooked vegetables or fruit broken down in a blender

**Purification** The process of making something or someone clean

**Purim** A Jewish holiday in memory of when the Jewish people were saved from a cruel man called Haman

**Qur'an** The Islamic holy book

**Raksha Bandhan** A Hindu festival that celebrates the relationship between brothers and sisters

**Ramadan** A month when Muslims hold a fast during the hours of daylight to become closer to Allah, and to remember the time that the Qur'an was first revealed to the Prophet Muhammad

**Resolution** A decision to do, or not do something

**Samhain Eve** A pagan festival for giving thanks at the end of the harvest

**Satellite** An object in space that orbits the Earth

**Sea Sunday** The day when Christians pray for sailors and their families

**Seder** A special Jewish feast to celebrate the beginning of Passover

**Shavuot** A Jewish holiday to remember the day that God gave Moses the Torah

**Shrove Tuesday** The day before the Christian period of fasting called Lent begins, also known as 'Pancake Day'

**Sikh** Someone who follows the religion of Sikhism and believes in the writings and teachings of the Ten Sikh Gurus

**Spring tide** A tide just after a new or full moon, when the difference between high tide and low tide is at its highest

**Swan Upping** An annual ceremony in which mute swans are taken from the River Thames to be counted and marked to identify them, before being released

**Synagogue** The Jewish place of worship

**Ten Commandments** A list of laws or rules that Christians and Jews follow that they believe were given by God to Moses

**Tide** The rising and falling of the sea

**Torah** The Jewish holy book

**Trooping the colour** A ceremony performed to celebrate the Queen's birthday

**Tu B'Shevat** Jewish New Year, also known as the 'New Year for Trees'

**Twelfth Night** A festival some Christians celebrate to mark the coming of the Epiphany

**Wassailing** A pagan tradition of blessing the apple trees in the new year

**Whitsun** Another name for the Christian festival of Pentecost

**Yom Kippur** A Jewish holiday for saying sorry for things you have done wrong and asking for forgiveness

**Yule** A pagan festival held in midwinter to celebrate the winter solstice

# INDEX